PRAISE

Firmly rooted in landscape and community, the essays of Erica Watson's *The Ghost of Distant Trees* are wise and stunningly self aware. Watson is a sharp, unsparing observer and a penetrating thinker; literally and figuratively, she leaves no stone unturned as she travels from an Arizona girlhood to an Alaska womanhood. Watson has covered a great distance in a far country and brought back for us from that frontier the news we need to hear.

—JOE WILKINS author of *The Entire Sky* and *When We Were Birds*

This is the angular prose of a straight shooter. With an eye for industry politics and idiosyncratic rural characters, Erica Watson studies Alaska's most ubiquitous public face: Denali National Park. "It becomes a story about gravel," she writes with characteristic, no-nonsense flair. In matters of the park, as in matters of the heart, *Ghosts of Distant Trees* cuts through the hubbub and casts complexity with deliciously streamlined ambivalence.

—CORINNA COOK author of *Leavetakings* and *Permafrost is an Archive*

Alaska has drawn many dreamers to its landscapes—Erica Watson among them. In these essays centered around her work in Denali National Park, she interrogates, with incisive criticism and vulnerable storytelling, the reality out from the myth. Hers is a frame that implores us to see the larger systems that have shaped and are shaping this place she now calls home alongside the intimate, sometimes contradictory details that give the park its beauty. These essays explore how climate change, political upheaval, and declining infrastructure connects us all, even in those places wrongly considered "distant," and they do so with a tenderness of attention and care toward the lands, creatures, and communities depicted. Watson wonders, "If mine is a love story," and yes, *Ghosts of Distant Trees* is, indeed, a love story, one that contends with the complexity, loss, and labor that comes with finding oneself entangled with something to which we know we cannot lay claim but with which we still yearn to belong.

—SEAN ENFIELD author of *Holy American Burnout!*

With her immersive, deeply considered essays, Erica Watson proves to be one of Alaska's finest contemporary writers. *Ghosts of Distant Trees* is place-based writing at its best, blending observation and memoir with philosophy and attitude. Anyone who wishes to know what it's like to live at the edge of Denali National Park, or in the world today, will find Watson to be an informed and engaging storyteller.

—NANCY LORD former Alaska Writer Laureate and the author of *Fishcamp* and *Early Warming*

To a visitor, "gateway town" connotes the scenic entrance to a National Park. When you live in such a place, it's a more complicated term, as "sublime" abuts "mundane." Erica Watson grew up in an NPS family and lives near Denali National Park, on Dene lands. In these insightful essays, she lays open the nuance that decades in a subculture can bring: wolves and wonder and quiet, and also abortions and elections, gravel pits and noise. "I always find myself drawn back into the in-between areas," Watson writes. By turns researched and intimate, questing and irreverent, Watson digs into the in-between glossed over by promotional campaigns and offers stories of living on land, among neighbors and beings, at the edge of the still-wild world. A unique and grounded voice in Alaska's vibrant non-fiction chorus.

—CHRISTINE BYL author of *Dirt Work and Lookout*

Watson reexamines easy narratives about place and belonging. She searches for fissures that point towards the tensions and joys of inhabiting unsettled geographies. From that vantage point, she describes scenes that would otherwise be overlooked, stretches of gravel, the after hours of tourist traps. In forgoing established eco-narratives, Watson allows us to dwell alongside her as she questions how landscapes have shaped her and the communities she belongs to.

—ANNIE WENSTRUP author of
The Museum of Unnatural Histories

A propulsive and timely collection, both deeply personal and widely significant—and especially urgent in this moment when our national parks are under existential threat.

—MANJULA MARTIN author of *The Last Fire Season*

Erica Watson's debut collection, *Ghosts of Distant Trees*, is as beautifully rendered as it is timely. Through this gathering of essays, Watson encourages readers to perceive with greater clarity while she cultivates a sense of self wholly immersed in landscape. In demonstrating an intimate understanding of place, Watson does not shy away from what is challenging, but provides us with an example to learn from as community members who exist, and resist, within late capitalism. With rich and evocative prose, Watson urges us to identify the complex relationships between the human and nonhuman and consider, then, the impact we—through the choice of action or inaction—make upon the environment around us, asking: "If, like [Wendell] Berry says, a road is laid in the wound prepared for it, is damage to a road an act of healing or further injury?" Watson's *Ghosts of Distant Trees* is a collection I will gratefully return to in the months and years ahead, as Watson's work exhibits both critical reflection and a grounded, radical practice of hope.

—TARA BALLARD author of *House of the Night Watch*

GHOSTS OF DISTANT TREES

GHOSTS OF DISTANT TREES

ERICA WATSON

Published November 2025 by Porphyry Press
Post Office Box MXY
McCarthy 22B
Glennallen, Alaska 99588
https://porphyry.press/

Book design by Krista West.
Text in Adobe Jensen Pro Caption.
Copyediting by Joeth Zucco.
Cover design incorporates Sara Tabbert's artwork, "In Cold Shadow," as photographed by Sarah Lewis.
Author photo by Craig Brandt.

LIBRARY OF CONGRESS CATALOGING-IN-PUBLICATION DATA ON FILE
Library of Congress Control Number: 2025944865
First Edition
ISBN 978-1-7367558-5-3 (paperback)
ISBN 978-1-7367558-6-0 (e-pub)

When you start on a long journey,
trees are trees, water is water,
and mountains are mountains.

After you have traveled some distance,
trees are no longer trees,
water no longer water,
mountains no longer mountains.

But after you have traveled a great distance,
trees are once again trees,
water is once again water,
mountains are once again mountains.

—Variant on Zen teaching,
first attributed to Master Qingyuan,
1252

CONTENTS

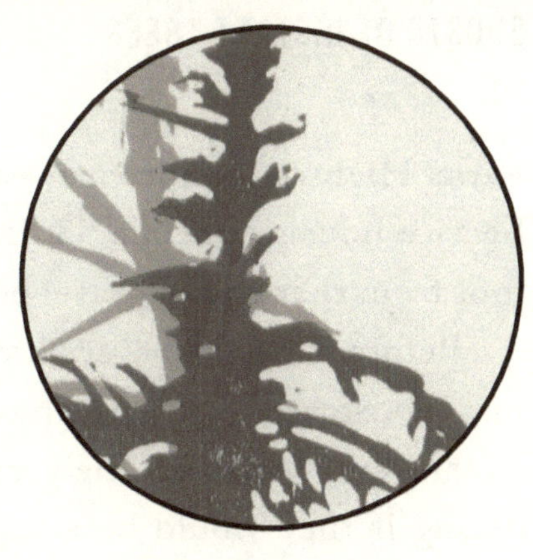

THE POSTCARD DAYS

Before flying north for a summer job halfway through college, what I knew about Denali National Park was that it was remote and big and had bears and one gravel road. Soon after arriving, I found myself with an unremarkable job in a remarkable place. Working forty hours a week selling books and postcards at the visitor center at mile 66 of said road—measured from its intersection with the

Parks Highway to the east—and living in National Park Service housing at mile 53. Everything not accessible on foot from that line of gravel began to fade from my mind.

Before it became everyday life, it felt like I'd stepped into a postcard. Not with any grace or majesty but a haphazard entry, eyes on the ground or on my shoes, wondering if they would be adequate for the situation; old battered headphones and an anachronistic ballad in my ears; and when I finally looked up, a dazed awe, as if the postcard had painted itself around me.

In the center of the postcards I sold, or sometimes slightly to the left or right, depending on the creativity of the photographer, loomed a four-mile-tall mound of snow-covered granite. This mountain, Denali, is the highest peak in North America, rising 20,310 feet from the tundra. The Koyukon word *Denali* is one of several local Indigenous names translated to mean "the high one" or "big mountain," and even from more than a hundred miles away the mountain's appearance on the horizon can set the scale of an image. The six-million-acre wilderness park bearing the mountain's name draws masses of tourists, backpackers, researchers, and seasonal workers like me and is made more accessible than other big Alaska national parks by its location on the highway and railroad. By the time I arrived in 2004, most of the stories told about the place highlighted the heroic exploits of prospectors, mountaineers, homesteaders, conservationists, and tourism entrepreneurs, rather than the "quiet reverence" shown to the mountain by Dene people who have lived in the forests and watersheds surrounding Denali for generations.

But a postcard image does not demand a context. Again and again, I sketched the mountain's well-documented contours from the visitor center thirty-three miles away, until I could draft a recognizable ridgeline with my eyes closed, the same ridgeline thousands had come to know the same way from the same location. Part of the daily duties in the visitor center included drawing the day's view of the mountain in a poster-sized calendar on the wall, so visitors could see how many rainy or clear days preceded them. This task rotated between Park Service naturalists, maintenance staff, and me. Often, the day's calendar square was left white, meaning low fog, rain, or sometimes dense wildfire smoke obscured the postcard view. On days like that, some visitors photographed the postcards or equally picturesque book covers, to prove they'd been there. There were plenty of duplicate photos to choose from; visitors started flocking to this location in 1939, and the aesthetic of how to frame the mountain doesn't seem to have evolved much.

In the foreground, a wide gray-brown plain, shaped by the braided Thorofare River, was broken in places into sparkling strands and shards by light on water—when the sun shone. To feel like a postcard, the sun had to at least partially shine. Out of the photo's frame was a patch of green tundra sloping up to where I sat on a splintery picnic table waiting for a bus, and the man driving it, most Sunday evenings, the start of my weekend that summer.

The bus I waited for took people deep into the park, dropping off backcountry campers along the way and stopping for the night at Wonder Lake Campground, another postcard spot twenty miles northwest along the Denali Park Road. Jeff, the driver, told me later that his early interest in me was sparked by the fact that I was so damn easy to please: "You wanted to see Alaska, and I could drive you into a gravel pit and tell a good story, and you'd be satisfied. It took almost no effort." He was right. I was twenty and had not yet developed desires beyond weekend road trips to obscure gravel pits outside the frames of the postcards I sold (and bought) for twenty-five cents. I played Joan Baez's *The First Ten Years* on repeat that summer, and the song "No Expectations" loops through all these memories: the narrator always coming or going, loving and losing, no expectation to return. I'd just finished my second year of college in southern Arizona and sought respite from what I'd eventually understand as burnout after two years of exhausting student activism against an ongoing war and ongoing economic system. The trip to Alaska had been on something of a whim. There'd been no investment, no stated goals, just something that had nothing to do with what I had been doing. Mark a dot on a map, take a picture, thank the man who brought you there. Easy.

Sometimes visiting hikers waited with me for the bus. Sometimes I talked to them. I tried to imagine us into vastly different worlds, mine defined by a perceived intimate acquaintance with the shadows on Denali as seen from this picnic table and the front seat of the bus, where I would firmly plant myself behind Jeff as soon as he pulled in. I imagined the park road then as a kind of workers' utopia, where everyone had a role, whether transporting people, gravel, or messages back and forth; sharing information about road conditions or wildlife sightings; trading snacks or gossip at rest stops. I knew that my own role was among the most expendable, so I made it my practice to collect facts and stories, bits of information to make myself relevant. I didn't want a job with responsibility, but I wanted to be near those who did.

My first night in the sixteen-foot trailer where bus drivers spent the night, I brought a sleeping bag but didn't use it. Easy to impress. It was early August, just dark enough to see hints of stars. I insisted on leaving the curtains open in case the northern lights came out, imagining them bright enough to wake me through the small, screened window.

Mornings came early in those trailers. The driver's shift started with an 8 a.m. departure from the Wonder Lake Campground for a pickup at the end of the road in Kantishna, then an immediate turnaround back east down the entire ninety-two-mile length of the road to the park entrance. Jeff suggested I stay near the lake and pick blueberries, and he'd pick me up on the return trip.

"I'll go with you," I said. "I haven't been to Kantishna yet."

"I'd kind of rather you didn't," he stuttered. "Strange things happen to me in Kantishna."

"What kinds of things?" I asked. I still sat in bed, intrigued by Jeff's idiosyncrasies, by the already bright sun streaming through the window at 6 o'clock, by my own ability to pretend this was something I did all the time.

He spread food out on the cramped table that folded down from the trailer wall. "Um. Aliens. Breakfast?" he said, proffering instant oatmeal, a nectarine, a handful of blueberries, and a glance at his watch.

I did what I was told. I went out to the road and picked berries till Jeff and his dusty green bus rolled back over the hills from Kantishna. The berries bounced into mush in the half-full Tupperware for the next four and a half hours as we drove east, and we ate them the next morning at his cabin in Healy, the tiny town on the northern boundary of the park.

The first time I *really* looked into a clear channel of the Toklat River, the image of water flowing over glacial sediment became firmly intertwined with Joan Baez's voice in my Discman, tucked into the pocket of my rain jacket, and the throbbing headache of an underage hangover, which was why I was kneeling by the river in the first place. The rocks ranged from fingernail-sized pebbles to freshly broken sandstone, cleaved evenly like sliced strips of steak, and rocks large enough to use as stepping stones formed bridges at intervals along the creek.

I didn't hear Jeff's bus pull in, and he'd crouched next to me before I saw him. These meetings along the park road were routine by now. I picked up stones and put them down again, and still not knowing how to talk to men, I informed him that as a kid, I'd named rocks and had invented complicated societies and biographies for them. It had seemed as plausible as giving life to a doll, and rocks were more reliably available. My problem, then, was that I became attached to rocks collected in campsites on family trips to national parks, and my father, a career park ranger, reminded me that I had to leave them where I found them. This left families of rocks separated, social conflicts unresolved.

In the children's book, *Everybody Needs a Rock*, Byrd Baylor gives instructions on finding your own special rock. "If somebody says, 'What's so special about that rock?' don't even tell them," she writes. "Nobody is supposed to know what's special about another person's rock."

As for finding your special rock, Baylor writes that there are rules. The first rule: "If you can, go to a mountain made out of nothing but a hundred million small shiny beautiful roundish rocks. But if you can't, anyplace will do. Even an alley. Even a sandy road."

One night after a day of selling postcards and drawing the weather, I walked alone for hours on the Toklat River bar, giddy at my surroundings: the muddy torrents of the Toklat flowing north from the peaks of the Alaska Range, the midnight sun on the peaks filtered to an orange glow by ubiquitous wildfire smoke that had settled in the Toklat River valley on still nights. Despite the smoke, I felt a boundless energy I haven't felt since, something unique to the liminality of being twenty on a glacial river bar in the middle of the night. I had only to show up at a mindless job the next morning. Time and river seemed infinite.

I walked north toward the sun, kneeling to touch an occasional rock or flower, scanning the horizon for movement: bears or unexpected humans. (Another night, I hid behind a granite boulder, squinting at the far bank of the river bar, trying to identify the strange shapes I saw moving there. I jumped with embarrassment when I realized it was a low tan tent and a person crouching to pee. I had to remind myself that my evening walks were other people's wilderness escape, and I resolved to get new glasses.) At my feet, the wet rocks sparkled, and one caught my eye. About the width of two fingers, slightly flattened with an indentation on one side, it looked vaguely like a misshapen heart. Black with white striations, the side facing up bore a mark like a miniature human footprint.

I picked it up and held it a while, intending to eventually throw it in the river. Instead, it spent the night on the bookshelf next to my bed at the road camp, footprint facing up. The rock ended up coming with me to Arizona that fall, though not casually, as I was still wracked with Park Service guilt. I built a mythology around it: the rock had to return to the Toklat, and until it did, no departure from Denali would be permanent. Once it was back in the river, I could leave for good if I wanted to.

Jeff eventually told me about the Kantishna aliens. Once, in dense fog and presumed solitude, he found himself separated from his then girlfriend by a small herd of migrating caribou with partially shed bloody velvet hanging in strings from their antlers, the bones in their hooves clicking against each other. He said that as they moved past him, they looked like human skeletons dripping blood. Though they knew that they were only fall caribou en route to the rutting grounds, both he and his companion were shaken by the grotesque image when they found each other again in the fog.

On another day, cloudless and radiant, trying to decide whether he and his partner would continue their relationship or part ways, a man known locally as the Cosmic Commander fell into step with them across the tundra. The three of them sat down, cross-legged, knee-to-knee, eyes on the mountain. The man, a holdout from the pre–National Park mining days who claimed to communicate with celestial beings while walking the park road, balanced a handgun on his knee and rocked it back and forth. He said he was communicating with the beings now, and they were on their way.

"What a weird fucking day," Jeff said, as four aircraft swept in from the north, the roar of their engines blocking all conversation.

The relationship had ended, and by the time I showed up he was reluctant to bring dates to Kantishna again. And so, for years, the place held a supernatural edge for me, too, even after Jeff and his aliens shifted away from the center of my world—slowly filling the map with stories, other people's ghosts, complicated messes that couldn't fit in a postcard no matter how it was framed. By the end of the summer, I was sketching flying saucers hovering over Denali's South Peak like lenticular clouds on the visitor center weather calendar.

The following January, when the Denali bookstore manager called asking if I wanted the job back that summer, I was hurriedly writing a paper between classes in Tucson. Other possibilities included working through the Sonoran summer as a barista, or trying to garner enough enthusiasm for a professional internship to apply for one. In a way the answer was easy: go where I was wanted, where I could get paid mostly to read books behind the counter with no bosses around. That year, I convinced a college acquaintance to come work with me, and she remains one of my closest friends, our lives intertwined across geographies. At the end of the second summer, I left boxes in friends' sheds in the communities surrounding the park and returned for other seasonal park jobs after tiring of postcard sales, even as I insisted that my "real life" would start elsewhere, someday soon.

Inevitably, other federally protected rocks came into my possession. As an act of courtship and apparently unaware of the psychic burden it would represent, a man once sent me a piece of petrified wood he'd found the previous summer on Polychrome Mountain, a roadside ridge in the park. It was midwinter, and Denali seasonals were scattered across the globe, thinking fondly of the

Alaska summer. The petrified wood sat on display on my desk in Tucson, then in a dry log cabin I rented for a time on Denali's edge, until it was tossed in a box or into the woods. I didn't feel bound by it, not like the black-and-white footprint rock.

For years, the rock lived in my purse or backpack, and it became a private ritual to wash it in waters around the world. It traveled the length of the Grand Canyon on the Colorado River; bathed in the Pacific and Atlantic Oceans, two Patagonian rivers, the Ganges, and a tributary of the Indus. Standing in long lines, I'd sometimes take it in my hand, move it between my fingers. And every summer I returned to Denali, it didn't seem right to leave it just yet.

It's not quite right to say Denali lost its magic, but perhaps it's truer to say the frame shifted. My ability and willingness to flirt my way onto any bus or dump truck changed with policy and age. As I settled into the community along the highway, outside the park, travel to Kantishna was limited not because of aliens or armed men who spoke to them but because of the hours and permits it required. The realities of union negotiations and concessions contracts disrupted my utopian vision of worker relations on the road. Returning from almost anywhere else to Denali offered a stark reminder of the overwhelmingly white park community's racial homogeneity. Any given social gathering was a collection of everyone's exes. The landscape no longer looked like postcard images, peopled by quirky characters and charming coincidences, but by life, often muddy, dusty, or impossibly frozen. I acquired furniture, emotional baggage, a small town reputation based first on years of chasing men along the park road and later as a civic-minded flake with a knack for cooking Mexican (by rural white Alaska standards). I became harder to impress.

But moments of radiant beauty still took my breath away. Once, returning to my rental cabin on the bluff above the Nenana River late on a cloudless, subzero night, the full moon and stars illuminated the valley in shades of blue; ice crystals reflected off every surface. I don't know how long I stood at the top of the steep, slippery path to my cabin watching and feeling that if that were my last moment on earth, it would be enough. When I finally went inside, I didn't turn on my single light for some time. I built a fire by the moonlight shining through the window and sat in awe as the cabin slowly warmed.

The night before I lost the footprint rock, I'd pulled it out of one bag to put it in another and told my travel companion, Craig, about its history. We were on vacation in Costa Rica, our first trip together outside Alaska.

He also worked at Toklat in the summers as a heavy equipment mechanic for the National Park Service. We'd been friends since my first summer, but I'd only recently moved from my rental cabin to his house. I told him I planned to wash the rock in some Costa Rican waters the next day, and by habit placed it in the hip strap pocket of the daypack I was sure I'd have with me for the remainder of the trip.

And I would have, if not for a series of dumb mistakes. The next day, forgetting for a moment that we weren't in Alaska, we saw an inviting waterfall just off the road and pulled over to dash to it for a quick swim. After days of what I felt was excessive caution, we left our two day packs visible on the seat of the rental car, against the wisdom of *Lonely Planet* and every American tourist before us. We returned to the car to find the driver's side window smashed with a grapefruit-sized rock, which sat on the car's console surrounded by broken glass. Both packs were gone.

The contents of my pack were mostly replaceable or unimportant. Craig's passport was in his bag, which necessitated what was for both of us a first visit to an American embassy, but within a day and a half we were back on the road. But more than the binoculars and the sweater, the loss of the footprint rock haunted me. I hoped that, after realizing its lack of worth, the thieves threw the pack's contents into the river.

I returned home without the footprint rock for the first time. Home now meant forcing my embarrassingly sunburnt legs into bunny boots and shoveling the snow that had fallen in our absence. It meant still tripping clumsily on my own feet as I looked up at the sky, not a scene from a postcard, but of a life, imperfect and always shifting.

Somewhere in the back of my mind, I still heard Joan Baez, singing someone else's song until it became her own.

CORDILLERA

As a kid, I pored over maps. I memorized state capitals and national flags. I was drawn to the way symbols made the abstraction of state lines and political power into tangible shapes and contours, the way a twisted and half-fallen barbed wire fence was made into a neat black line on paper.

My first maps included a colorful three-dimensional plastic puzzle of the contiguous United States, and I learned the shapes of the states I'd lived in (three by the time my family landed in Arizona when I was six), the states where my parents lived before I was born (three and four, two together), where our relatives lived (the Midwest, mostly), and which states bordered each of them (flat ones, mostly). I liked that Arizona's combination of straight lines and jagged, riverine edges distinguished it from its Four Corners neighbors. I learned that each piece could be categorized by topography alone; even with closed eyes, it was clear from the wrinkled plastic mountains if a state belonged to the western or eastern half of the puzzle. I knew which half I preferred.

Another favorite map depicted Wupatki National Monument, the small National Park Service site where my family first lived in northern Arizona. The minimalist map in the glossy brochure handed out to tourists outlined the irregular shape of the monument, boundaries determined by locations of Ancestral Puebloan dwellings that it was established to protect. National Park Service, National Forest Service, Navajo Nation, and private ranchlands were color coded and clearly delineated on the map. The main roads, Highway 89 to the west and the paved road connecting Wupatki and neighboring Sunset Crater National Monument, drew a D-shaped loop in black and red and omitted the network of dirt forest roads and off-road-vehicle trails I knew existed on the land, if not the map. In my young imagination, the rigidity of these printed lines represented truth despite the obvious impermanence of fences, the way a sheep or cow had no regard for grazing law, the strangeness of a white kid like me calling Wupatki home, even though my only living grandparent lived in Ohio, my ancestry European.

Sometimes I drew detailed insets to accompany my copy of the government-issued brochure, which included the places I knew best: our house and the three other residential buildings, maintenance yard, and visitor center that closely neighbored us, and the trail leading from the visitor center to the partially stabilized pueblo behind it. My versions included the loosely cobbled sandstone footpath between the visitor center and our front yard, and every notably shaped large stone slab I played on. I liked the quiet entitlement of walking past the Authorized Use Only sign on the path to the house. I liked the feeling of being a part of the place in a way I imagined the tourists did not.

Years later, I'd read Edward Abbey's essay "A Walk in the Park," an account of walking with his nine-year-old daughter to the site of a then proposed road in southern Utah. When asked by her father why she thought no road should be built, preventing the "too old, too young, too fat, too thin, scared, ignorant, rich or poor" from getting to the place, she replied, "Everybody can't have everything." When asked if she thought she was "better than most people," the child replied, "Well, a little bit better."

I liked spying on tourists in a game my younger brother and I called "visitoring," which started with a slow belly crawl into the narrow concrete drainage ditch behind the visitor center, just deep enough to conceal our small bodies. We inched our way past the visitor center, pausing at the restroom windows. If our presence silenced conversation or if we heard words like "What are those kids doing out there?," we lost and returned to the house to start a new round.

But if we made it past the restrooms, we continued to the fenced garden where the rangers tried to grow corn twelfth-century-style in the mix of sand and volcanic cinder, and from there, it was a short distance to the trailside juniper bush where we could observe visitors undetected. Transcending the rules and the map was among the perks afforded to the boss's kids.

It was my dad's job to enforce the law within Wupatki's designated boundaries. At times this meant ticketing someone speeding on the winding paved loop road or recovering a pocketed nine-hundred-year-old pottery shard that had found its way to the surface and if left alone would disappear again with the next rain. Sometimes it meant moving a sheep or a cow that crossed a mapped line reinforced by barbed wire. The law also regulated how descendants of the people who built the structures that the monument protects could visit and practice millennia-old traditions on federally managed lands. In a 1999 press release—years after we'd moved from Wupatki to Flagstaff—addressing ongoing legal disputes about certain

Hopi ceremonial practices within monument boundaries, the director of the Hopi Cultural Preservation Office said, "We question [the ability of the National Park Service] to be good caretakers of our ancestral villages." In those moments, I gradually came to understand that a map is often a work in progress and that it matters who draws the lines.

Early one morning, still in pajamas, orange juice in hand, I surveyed the desert landscape through the front door windows. The Painted Desert stretched to the east, the reds and rusts of Coconino sandstone faded to blue in the distance, eighty-mile visibility on a clear day. I liked this fact, knowing the distance from our porch to the Hopi Buttes on the horizon. On this day, though, something else caught my eye.

"There's a boat on the flagpole," I announced. The visitor center next door to our house was not yet open for the day. At the top of the flagpole, a boat and a figure standing in it hovered over the empty parking lot at a height that boats did not belong.

"What the . . ." said my dad and then went for his uniform, green, gray, and a gun on his hip.

"I heard something squeaking earlier," I said. Maybe I had heard something from my bed on the other side of the small house, metal scraping metal as the boat ascended. Or maybe I just liked to be the one to know things, a seven-year-old authority on all local events.

My dad left to alert his colleagues and investigate. My mom, brother, and I watched from the window. Soon we learned that the figure in the boat was JD. We knew him the way everyone knows everyone in national parks, as a friendly maintenance worker who offered horse-drawn buggy rides to the kids at park holiday parties and had a history of using public lands as the backdrop for his theatrical criticisms of the agencies and the nation that managed them.

It was Presidents' Day weekend at the start of the first Gulf War. The flagpole swayed whenever JD moved in his boat.

I knew the flagpole well. It was taller than the stocky silver-colored poles at school, and it was painted sandstone pink to match the landscape. Whenever I could, I'd run down at the end of the rangers' evening shifts and help them fold the sheet-sized American flag into a neat triangle. They often closed the visitor center alone, and the help of a kid who really liked folding cloth meant they didn't have to lay the flag down on the floor and hope no one saw. I liked helping. I liked the rules, the importance of the stars-on-the-outside and the never-touch-the-ground. I liked the ritual. But mostly I just liked folding things.

JD had rigged a rope-and-pulley system, not unlike the rope used to raise and lower the flag every day, to hoist his small orange rowboat almost to the top. The boat was labeled "Bush Boat" in black letters. When my dad and the sheriff from town went up in a cherry picker to negotiate, they learned that JD's box to poop in was labeled "Bush box." JD wore his government-issued flat hat with a fake mushroom planted on top. He also flew a flag, stars and stripes upside down and blowing in the wind. This meant America was in trouble. It also meant JD was in trouble.

He dropped a dummy in a noose out of the boat and called it Bush, and it swung back and forth whenever JD stood up. When he put a second noose around his own neck, I wasn't allowed to watch anymore. My dad and the others took all the mattresses from all the houses down to the base of the flagpole in case he jumped, and put metal trash cans upside-down over the posts.

He did not jump.

He did not spend long in jail.

He did not come back to work for the National Park Service, or stop the war.

The morning JD raised his boat, the buttes on the horizon were obscured by winter haze, flat light, and no shadows.

Comparisons between JD and Edward Abbey were inevitable. The subtitle to the *Arizona Daily Sun* article reporting on one of JD's more recent sentencings—five years' probation for blocking a mountain bike race in the Coconino National Forest reads, predictably, "No More Monkeywrenching."

Following several suicides among our peers, my friends and I formed a film club my senior year of high school in Flagstaff and set out to make a short film meant to hold ourselves and each other to the living world.

That school year had started with my first boyfriend breaking up with me a second time, this time by the advice of a tarot card, followed immediately by the September 11 attacks and subsequent calls for nationalist retaliation. I attended peace rallies in downtown Flagstaff and wrote angry poems. The first boy I'd kissed, a summer music camp romance years earlier, called me upon returning from deployment in Afghanistan to tell me he thought anyone protesting the war should be executed. I fought with school administrators about the Pledge of Allegiance, visible bra straps, the requirement that I pass a math class. I was a live wire and bored with it. The suicide victims were each friends of friends or acquaintances, not my own close circle, but the ripples of each death were inescapable. At school, teachers checked in on me in ways that suggested they thought I might be next. I appreciated their concern but felt confident that anyone in real danger wouldn't be so obvious about it, all black eyeliner and heartbreak poems on morning announcements. I wavered daily between intense defensiveness of my friends and their losses and a desire to isolate from them completely. The film project offered a structure for our collective grief that allowed us to talk about it at a slant, in terms of art and technicalities: a camera angle, a line of dialog.

We shot melancholy scenes in someone's parents' unfurnished investment property, in the ponderosa forests surrounding town, along the train tracks, and in downtown buildings, where our most difficult scene was set. In a flashback, the ghost who returned to encourage a young man having suicidal thoughts to seek healing showed him her own death.

We convinced the management of a historical downtown hotel to grant us roof access day after day so we could capture the perfect shot of a life-size dummy falling from the roof. My role included keeping the dummy prepped for another fall, which meant pinning its wig back in place and stuffing its jeans full of rags to best match the size and figure of the actor. Sometimes this was all we did, all afternoon, while waiting for the director—a teenager with a clear artistic vision but limited social power—to gain access to another roof for yet another angle.

Our footage was often marred by bored cops chanting "Jump! Jump! Jump!" from the sidewalk below, and me and the rest of the rooftop crew shouting back at them. The dummy once lost its wig in a tree midfall, and we had to reshoot after retrieving it with the hotel's broom handles. We spent hours recreating this fictional death, losing track of the rest of the script and the filming schedule we'd set for ourselves. Most of us were graduating in spring, and other tasks took priority as the date neared. We never finished the project.

Some days, though, as winter ended and the high desert sun returned in full strength, we just laid around on the roof together, a group of teenage misfits and our imaginary ghost's body double, talking about who we planned to be when this was over.

I intended to be more transient than I came to be, more spontaneous road trips with strangers than alphabetized bookshelves, more migratory, more white-crowned sparrow than ptarmigan.

But immediately after high school, I traveled only as far as Tucson, to study at the University of Arizona. I didn't have a car, so depended on others for any road trips, but traveling the dusty city by bicycle quickly grew on me. I liked feeling close to the elements; once, I mistimed a ride from campus to work and waited out a late season monsoon with a real estate agent who invited me and my bike onto the small steps of his office. We watched in shared awe as the poorly drained street turned briefly to river and back again. My heat tolerance skyrocketed. I mapped out narrow alleys as shortcuts and felt liberated by not having to think about parking lots or permits.

That year had an edge to it, too, the threat of war in a distant desert looming. I joined weekly anti-war demonstrations at the downtown federal building, carrying posterboard signs rolled under my arm as I biked from class to my tutoring job to the busy sidewalk at rush hour. I marched and chanted and tabled with activist student groups, pretended to die in protest in the university cafeteria, and sometimes thought of JD, wondering why he hadn't chosen to hang his Bush Boat in front of city hall or at a busy street corner instead of a remote parking lot in the Painted Desert. Still, even as these often arbitrary actions to stop the United States from bombing Iraq took up almost all my free time and energy, I had a sense that maybe the specifics didn't matter; that the most measured and strategic or the most incoherent acts of protest would fail to sway policy, so you might as well go for theatrics.

The day the US invasion of Iraq began, I was in Ottawa, Canada, spending my first college spring break visiting a friend from high school who took advantage of his Canadian citizenship to study there. I convinced him to attend the march on the parliamentary building and to briefly entertain the possibility of marrying me as an act of (my) protest against the United States. But at the end of the week, we were both pragmatists and still had classes to go to. My friend also knew, as a member of a Canadian First Nation, that the difference between the two nations was largely one of optics.

And if I'd learned anything from JD, it was this: find the place where you are most known, and stand there.

The war and the activism that surged in its wake in the early 2000s drew new lines on my maps, connecting the Raytheon missile plant in Tucson to civilians killed in Iraq, connecting Arizona's state spending to incarcerations around the US, connecting migrant deaths in the borderlands desert to the global north's exploitive trade policies. I started to understand that the warnings I'd grown up with of radioactive water in the Little Colorado River near Wupatki exist in the context of the weapons industry's ongoing legacy in the Navajo Nation. The water was safe (if awful tasting) on the monument side of the boundary but not across the river. I started to see maps as acts of imagination or longing rather than fact and understood that it was important to ask whose imagination a map depicted.

I helped friends prepare to block trucks hauling missiles from the manufacturer to the military base. I accompanied others on midnight trips to Walmart to buy U-locks to lock themselves to the university administration to demand that they no longer invest in private prisons. I attended community workshops on how to administer at-home abortions, in case legal access was ever threatened, a pursuit that felt more performative than practical at the time. I stood around backyard bonfires while others burned flags, supportive in theory and bored in practice. For my friends, I wrote zines about bikes and clouds and the joys of small rocks but struggled to translate any of this energy into my undergrad poetry classes. I felt the now familiar pull between everything and nothing, the chaos of connection and the peace of isolation.

When I told a former teacher who had become a friend about these feelings of burned-out restlessness, she suggested seasonal work at Denali National Park in Alaska, where she'd spent the summer before. It sounded like an easy enough escape. Seasonal jobs were easy to come by and easy to leave. I'd spent summers in high school working at the national monument bookstores around Flagstaff. I knew the language of national parks.

As I finished my second year as an undergraduate and the idea of Alaska took hold of my imagination, it was an Alaska devoid of politics, history, and connections across boundaries. Amy Clary, a scholar I'd later meet at Denali who always kept at least one foot outside the academic world, wrote about this American literary tradition of (un)mapping, using, as a case study, the popularity of Jon Krakauer's *Into the Wild*, which made famous the story of a privileged young man who starved to death in isolation near the boundary of Denali National Park in 1990. While he "may not have carried a physical map of the area's topography," Amy wrote, "nonetheless his path was clearly blazed by the books that informed his actions."

In the years that followed, we spoke often about the way these literary maps infused our experiences, even unconsciously, of all these lone white men with their tragedies and their confident politics and nothing to hold them to any one place. As I traveled between summer tourism seasons and school semesters, I fostered a romanticized kinship with migratory birds as an alternative to the literary tradition, the way they leave the north when snow falls and live an entirely different life in the desert, or in near-constant motion between continents, the way the shift in daylight makes them restless. I didn't learn the call of the white-crowned sparrow until I heard it in its northern breeding grounds at Denali and learned to see them in winter throughout the Southwest. I envied migratory birds' ability to take their cue and to know where to go next. I listened to folk songs about leaving and longing on repeat, white-crowned sparrows crossing borders, understanding performed mobility as part of settler colonial inheritance, at once compelled and exhausted by it.

An academic advisor showed me a map of Spanish-language study abroad programs with tuition matching. I traced the line of mountains south to the Andes, settling on a program in Buenos Aires that would allow time to see other parts of the country while completing a Spanish minor in only one semester, which at the time seemed like a practical counterbalance to my poetry and women's studies classes.

When I think of those six months in Buenos Aires, homesick for North American deserts and mountains and at a loss as to how to entertain myself in such a large city, I remember most my quiet pride when I successfully navigated the bus schedule, and the laughter-filled kitchen a young man I dated shared with his father and siblings, where someone had written the words "Apocalypso ahora . . . o más tarde" in Sharpie across the face of the clock on the wall, which ticked away the seconds of our short time together. And I think of long afternoons spent at the art museum, watching a looping video of a mirage on a Patagonian highway.

The video was part of an exhibit called *Historia de un disengaño*, (Story of a deception), by the Belgian Mexican artist Francis Alÿs. The book I bought about the exhibit explains that for Alÿs, the footage of the mirage represented "the lost tracks" of the nandú, or American rhea, and the Tehuelches, the people who hunted this flightless bird: something seen only from a distance, and gone if approached. "Hunting was done on foot across hundreds of kilometers until the bird was exhausted: the act of walking as weapon." Distance was what eventually killed the preyed-upon birds.

I don't recall any narration or soundtrack on the film, just a static whirring of the wind and a click of the projector when the segment restarted. A two-lane highway, split with a broken white line, yellowed grass of the pampas on both sides, a power line, a blur of movement obscuring the point where the road disappeared at the horizon. I occasionally brought friends to see it, gringos and locals, but I couldn't quite explain in English or Spanish what drew me back to it.

Alÿs describes walking as his medium, distance as his canvas. In another performance, he crossed the border between San Isidro and Tijuana by traveling south along the west coast of the Americas, flying from Tierra del Fuego to New Zealand and sailing between a chain of islands north to the Aleutians, eventually arriving in Southern California, undocumented, via Highway 101 South.

I spent my last afternoon in Buenos Aires eating cheesecake in a café with my boyfriend's sister. It was July, late winter in the Southern Hemisphere, and I had an overnight flight to Tucson, where I would do laundry and eat a burrito, and the following night another flight to Alaska. I didn't want to talk about it, so we talked instead about her art, Argentine politics, berries versus chocolate.

As we left the café to meet my boyfriend at the gallery where he worked, the steady rain turned to sheets, then to grape-sized hail. Ice piled up in the streets, and buses swerved to the curb when the drivers could no longer see. We ducked into a sporting goods store, and my friend shouted over the sound of ice hitting the roof that my flight would undoubtedly be canceled. "¡Es una catastrophe climática!" she said.

And it was, briefly. We huddled with strangers amid shelves stacked with soccer cleats in the doorway, watching vehicles slide out of control on accumulated hail. This is my sign, I thought. *I'm not supposed to leave.*

Then the hail stopped, just as quickly as it had started. Activity resumed in the streets. We reunited and rushed to make up for lost time in arranging my ride to the airport. I cried in the backseat of the cab for half the drive, then turned to look behind me as the airport neared. The setting sun reflected on the wet road ahead, but dense fog enveloped the city.

Midwinter in a Flagstaff bar with a man I'd met recently in a Wilderness First Responder course, I studied a massive framed geological map of Arizona. The heavily textured rust color representing the Colorado Plateau dropped away to the yellow and green basin and range of the south, placing the Mogollon Rim at about eye level. We'd just spent an aimless weekend driving around northern Arizona, drinking in dive bars in towns I hadn't been to since high school orchestra trips. We stopped at the north entrance to Wupatki on Highway 89, but we didn't drive the loop road or visit the pueblos. We talked about continuing farther north, to the states where we each had PO boxes and intentions to return, but we didn't. He had another course in Flagstaff to complete. My parents expected me for dinner.

"It's really an almost perfect map," I repeated, drawing his attention back to it again and again. He agreed to some objective truths like the dramatic elevation range and tragic shortsightedness of Lake Powell and ordered us another round. That was the winter I made up my mind to call Alaska home but hadn't fully convinced myself yet, slowly recognizing that there would be a loss either way.

Alÿs wrote that it is "the vanity of our intent that animates" the Patagonian mirages he chased, and "if there is disillusionment, it is because we want to catch it, to touch it."

Most ptarmigan, the year-round chicken-like residents of the northern tundra, don't migrate over great distances, instead traveling up and down mountain slopes with the seasons, following available food sources. They fly only when necessary.

To all accusations of excessive development the administrators can reply, as they will if pressed hard enough, that they are giving the public what it wants, that their primary duty is to serve the public not preserve the wilds.

—Edward Abbey
Desert Solitaire

Be patient toward all that is unsolved in your heart and try to love the questions themselves. . . . Perhaps you will then gradually, without noticing it, live along some distant day into the answer.

—Rainer Maria Rilke
Letters to a Young Poet

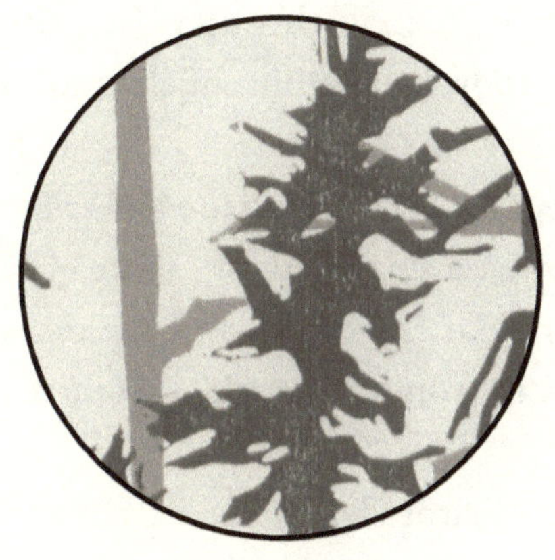

RENOVATION

1.

Jeff gave me a late night ride in his dump truck to the construction site where he was part of the crew building the new visitor center. It was two o'clock, after an August Mardi Gras party at the National Park Service road camp, and I hadn't been there in a year, before construction began. I'd told him I was curious to see the progress.

I hung my green and purple beads from the truck's rearview mirror as if staking a claim. I stood in the rain, glacial mud soaking through my socks and sandals, wearing a gold-sequin-covered polyester skirt from the five-dollar clothing rack at the Fairbanks Fred Meyer. The subarctic twilight cast a dim light on the mountains and thick ground-hugging fog. A silhouetted demolition crane hovered above me, and in the distance beyond it, the faint bluish outline of Denali through the mist. If I hadn't known where to look for the hint of the mountain, it would have been easy to miss.

Jeff backed up the truck and unloaded glacial river gravel into a pit. I stepped over the survey stakes that littered the ground. My throat tightened, and the tears surprised me. I looked away from the truck. I wished I had just gone to bed.

The original Eielson Visitor Center, where I'd worked a season selling books and postcards had been demolished, and construction for the new facility would take most of two more summers. The old building, built in the early sixties as part of a national attempt to modernize national park facilities, had jutted from the hillside at awkward, blocky angles. Some compared it to a hamburger stand. Biologist and naturalist Adolph Murie wrote in the April 1963 issue of *National Parks Magazine* that a couple visiting from Anchorage described the new building as "the Eielson monstrosity." The label "monstrosity" stuck, but it took on more affectionate overtones for those of us who came later, when its existence was no longer notable.

The visitor center provided a destination or a pit stop for visitors traveling the park road by bus, and on a sunny day the landscape overshadowed the scant services and exhibits. On rainy days it could feel like we were perched on small island in the clouds.

My first summer at Denali was that building's last in use. The men's bathroom was gradually detaching from the rest of the building as a result of years of earthquake damage, and the question of whether or not it would remain intact and upright faced each new group of arrivals. They may or may not all fit inside, and there may or may not be a comfortable place to sit. Some people wanted more luxurious facilities—coffee, collectors' spoons, phone service, functional heating—but they didn't get them. They had to go outside. They had to stand in the rain. Some of them hated it. Others took a walk.

I loved my ten-hour shifts watching them come and go from a wooden stool surrounded by books in the corner. I loved hiking in every direction from the visitor center on my days off, not yet concerned with things like staying dry or following a reasonable route. I'd return to the visitor center, my cotton clothes wet and muddy, and pore over geology and flower guides in the crowded linoleum-tiled display room until I was able to catch a bus back to Toklat, the Park Service road camp where I lived. I loved the chaos that ensued when a bear strolled into the parking lot, and the curmudgeonly ranger herded everyone into the small cinderblock-walled entryway and pulled closed a clanking metal gate around them, camera lenses poking through the holes. I loved being part of something so unapologetically outdated and ridiculous in such an iconic setting. I'd read Edward Abbey's *Desert Solitaire* and knew enough to be skeptical of so-called progress but not enough to be skeptical of Abbey.

Jeff and I didn't talk for several miles driving east to Toklat Road Camp. Free of the weight of gravel, the dump truck bounced on the washboard. It was dark now and still foggy.

"Do you feel anything?" I finally blurted out. Jeff concentrated on the barely visible turns in the road and the useless windshield wipers. "About that, I mean," I said, vaguely waving my hand behind us, in the direction of the Monstrosity. I picked at my sequins.

"I try not to," he said after a moment. "What good would it do?"

I didn't have an answer. We fell again into silence. Jeff had been driving this road as a bus driver for almost twenty years by then, and this year he had switched to the construction crew for a change of pace. He told me that it wasn't always easy for him to watch the crews tear up the tundra under the alpenglow of Denali, but it paid well, and more people means more infrastructure, everywhere. He enjoyed the creative processes of construction work, the satisfaction of completing a project.

The truck sped up with the gentle decline into the Toklat River valley. I leaned my head against the cold window and closed my eyes.

We rounded the last bend above the river. Jeff slammed on the brakes, and the truck clanked to a stop, metal hitting metal and the tires sliding on wet gravel. I jerked awake and saw something move in the willows through the mud-coated passenger-side window. The headlights shone first on two glowing yellow eyes and then on the figure of a gray wolf. We knew her from her frequent appearances on the road as the alpha female of the Grant Creek wolf pack. She was a strong hunter, and while her mate skittishly avoided the road, she sometimes trotted alongside buses for miles. She stood about ten feet in front of the truck, paused midstep in the road, and stared. "Hey you," I whispered dumbly. She held one foot in the air, ready to run. Jeff turned off the truck's engine, and then the headlights. The wolf kept staring at us, and I couldn't meet her eyes. She lowered her foot to the ground, and even as she slowly crossed the road, she kept watching us until she disappeared into the willows. A different kind of silence hung between us the remainder of the trip.

2.

Two years after standing in the mud at the construction site, I attended the grand opening of the new visitor center. The ceremony was held on a rare summer day when the sun shone in a cloudless blue sky, braided channels of the Thorofare River shimmered silver-white in the valley below, and the snow-covered peaks of the Alaska Range framed the ribbon-cutting ceremony. Chairs formed a half circle around the podium, where local and national dignitaries offered their blessings to the visitor center, talking big W Wilderness: a place the Wilderness Act says "man is only a visitor who does not remain," without permanent built structures. Government officials from Anchorage and Washington, DC, touted the building's low visual impact, half-buried in the hillside, use of local and recycled materials, and meticulously researched interpretive displays. Inside, recycled chipboard tables were loaded with platters of well-traveled chunks of melon and pineapple and cheese cut into stackable cubes.

A representative of the Department of the Interior from Washington, DC, quoted Richard Louv's *Last Child in the Woods*, in which a young child says he prefers to play inside rather than outside because "that's where all the outlets are." Places like this, a symbol of the wild, he said, are working against that sentiment. I remember thinking about the microphone and speaker system, but I don't remember extension cords or generators, and I don't know for sure where the outlets were.

As the dignitaries spoke, I leaned on the sun-warmed basalt walls, picked out a handful of pepperjack from the platter with a toothpick, and clapped at appropriate times. If there was a moment of silence, I've forgotten it. I had questions about some of the speakers' concepts of the relationship between a symbol and the thing it symbolized and the allowable distance between the two, but I guessed that maybe every recently graduated English major had those questions. The late Dene chief Mitch Demientieff told an origin story of the mountain, and I realized later with personal and collective embarrassment that he was the first Alaska Native person I'd seen speak at a National Park Service event in my four summers. The fact of his story's existence countered the narrative of the unpeopled wilderness, but because his ancestors had not built permanent structures in what is now the park's boundaries, their relationships to it were often minimized. Buildings or the lack of them carry so much weight.

After the ribbon cutting and the praise of the beautiful weather, I changed clothes in the spacious new restroom, equipped with low-flow toilets and hand dryers. And then I hiked west on the Thorofare River, away from the visitor center, which quickly faded from view: 7.4 million well-hidden government dollars tucked into the tundra. It is, indeed, a very nice building. From the river, it would be easy to miss, as intended.

On clear days like that, sunlight reflecting off the snow and ice on Denali can be almost blinding.

3.

It's difficult now to understand what I felt I'd lost with the old building. I did not plan a career selling postcards there, and I already knew I was not cut out for long-term National Park Service employment, either disseminating information and guiding hikes or cleaning the bathrooms. I did not anticipate spending much more time there at all.

I wonder if my reaction that night with Jeff was one of guilt disguised as grief. If, in seeing the holes in the tundra, the crane, and the dump truck, I was pushed to reckon with the impact of industrial tourism—the industry that shaped my days—on the landscape, but chose not to. Instead, I focused on the gravel and the man who hauled it there, as if we had not arrived together.

Another way to think about this perceived loss: Seeking transformation, I arrived in a place I knew nothing about. I was one of many who come here knowing nothing, part of a long legacy of uninformed newcomers. Some of those who came before had power that meant something far, far away. Others' stories have faded into the half-truth composites of pioneers and adventurers, caricatures and forgotten ghosts. It's not a legacy inclined to ask questions of itself or those who preceded it.

Denali National Park's official origin story often begins with the arrival of a well-connected East Coast hunter's pursuit of Dall sheep, the white sheep unique to northern mountains, in the early 1900s. He became enthralled with the sheep and their tundra habitat. This hunter and his contemporaries took their desires and dreams with them when they left and told their powerful friends in Washington, DC, what they'd seen: snow-capped peaks, green rolling hills where trees never grew, animals that didn't know to be afraid of humans, and other hunters who killed for money rather than prestige and whose excesses threatened to kill too many sheep before more people could see them. This faraway government drew lines on a map and called the hills and mountains theirs. The inclusion of Denali and other high peaks of the Alaska Range in the original two-million-acre park was almost incidental; the founding legislation names wildlife protection as the park's purpose.

In the 1920s, the newly formed National Park Service paid one person, then two, to stop other people from hunting too much. At first, they didn't build much either, just a few cabins, a dog kennel, an office. After a few years, when the Alaska Railroad reached the eastern boundary of the new park, construction began on the park road. It took a long time, and not a lot of people came to drive it. World War II meant even fewer people came, and many of the hunters left too. But after the war, people wanted jobs, others wanted vacations, and some of them wanted to feel like the world could still contain wonder and space and the sublime possibility that a wolf might look them in the eye and assure them that no, not all is lost.

And those people also needed a place to poop. And they had questions about the wolves. And the people who answered the questions and cleaned the bathrooms also needed places to poop, and sleep, and do paperwork, and fix the machines that built the road that the people traveled on.

In 1980, Congress passed the Alaska National Interest Lands Conservation Act (ANILCA), which expanded and established parks and preserves throughout Alaska and tripled the size of Denali National Park and Preserve. ANILCA is still considered a sweeping conservation victory by those who consider conservation legislation a victory, but it was met with local protest at the time. Up to a thousand people gathered in Cantwell, the small community that had grown around a Native village and railroad camp in the 1930s and was now situated on the then new eastern boundary of the preserve. Attendees camped for a weekend inside the boundary, collectively violating regulation. By most accounts, they had a good time.

But the new lines remained on the maps, the tourism industry gained social and economic traction, and Denali's draw as a destination grew. A lot of people who came on vacation or to work or for something in between had an idea that everything would stay the way it was when they first saw it. They brought with them the idea that history was a relatively recent phenomenon in this place. They brought books by people from other places who made whole careers and movements out of the idea that history began and ended with them. And then they brought more people who also didn't know much, but needed a way to make money from it because they wanted to stay.

It's a nuanced thing for a culture to define itself by disconnecting from the place in which it originated, and then to build a government agency and supporting industries around reestablishing a connection. Inevitably, contradictions abound: we extoll the virtues of a places left "untrammeled by man" while arguing for the necessity of upgraded facilities. We celebrate the purity and intrinsic value of the land on one side of a line while drilling, mining, or building up to the boundary on the other. I understand now how, in reckoning with these contradictions, it was easy to lose a sense of scale, to blame a single building when history is the problem. To not let a wolf just be a wolf, but to drag it into one's own tortured metaphor for permanence.

The no-longer-new building would, as predicted by the crew who built it, eventually flood with spring meltwater; the design prioritized its integration into the hillside over its ability to withstand the weather. After a series of anticipated and unanticipated events, water saturated the buried roof and walls. I didn't have much reaction to hearing this news. By the time it happened, there was so much else to have an opinion on. Besides, water always wins.

From the river below, it would be easy to miss that there was a building there at all.

END WORDS

For a college poetry workshop, I wrote a sestina about a person I never knew, someone who had been important in the past to someone who was important to me. When people spoke of her, their descriptions took on an almost mythological quality, and the details bore repeating: her soft-spoken expert knowledge of birds, her long blonde hair, and the haunted look in her eyes that drew people—men, women, gold miners, tourists—to her, and the fact that the last 'anyone' knew, she'd run away to live in a hole in the ground near the Arctic Circle with a militant secessionist miner.

"Do you want to go find her? Can we go visit?" I teased once, near a road junction north of Fairbanks where it might have been an option. "No, I don't, and we can't," was the decisive answer from my then lover, whose heart she had perhaps irreparably broken when she'd left fifteen years before. Her ghost joined us in the car.

When my undergraduate poetry workshop discussed my clumsy sestina, a hippie girl I often sat with in class leaned over and whispered, "I lived in a hole once."

"Yeah? How was it?" I imagined the Kantishna mining district as it had been described to me, in the final years of its late 1980s transition from pioneer outpost to tourist destination, and the tempting alternatives that might have been offered to an impressionable twenty-something Minnesotan blonde: a life closer to the land, less mediated by industry, with a man who claimed exemption from the rules.

I knew even less of this girl sitting next to me. Her poetry, like all of ours, was overpopulated with the wrong men, whiskey, and metaphors comprised of stray cats and rain. I pictured her in a dug-out pit in a Tucson backyard, strewn with cactus, cinderblocks, and cracked, sunbaked lawn chairs. "It was amazing," she said and looked at me like I was supposed to understand something. I nodded.

She turned back to the copy of my poem on her desk.

The sestina form repeats each line's end words from the first stanza in the five that follow, ordered in a way that the repetition could appear random without close attention. The form partially hides its pattern and also makes it inescapable, six words circling like ravens over a kill. I haven't written one since.

Years later, driving south from Fairbanks, my friend Nan told me stories from her early years at Denali. It was seventeen below and the noon sun barely cleared the snow-laden spruce lining the highway. Nan first worked in Kantishna in the '80s, where she fostered her passion for birds connected with others doing the same. The ghost appeared again.

"So you knew her too?" I asked. Nan always seemed to know everyone.

"Yeah, I haven't seen her for two or three years, but when we worked out in Kantishna, we were close, before she took off with Emmett," Nan said, about this woman who for me lived only in stories. "It's sad. They're living in pure squalor, in this shack, and it gets cold out there. Two kids, she can't afford to feed them, and Emmett's so anti-government he won't even let her get food stamps. Martha drops them food sometimes, but God, her eyes were sunken in and so skinny. She was trying to home-school the kids, but what they need is to get out. This is not the romantic dream of bush Alaska, it's just tragic, and man, is he a creepy, creepy guy." She trailed off. I couldn't think of any good questions.

In the poem, I had her name birds for eternity, and returning her to the hole at night at peace with her life, narrated in subtly repetitive and wholly unmemorable stanzas. I'd pictured her as the beautiful, lost girl my ex-lover met in college and convinced to come with him to Alaska. But in that moment this personal myth became a very real woman starving to death in the woods with two kids and an abusive man. The hole and all its figurative appeal collapsed, and in its place stood a poorly built wooden shack, surrounded by the usual snow-covered detritus of rural Alaska living.

Nan and I fell into silence. As the sun dropped again below the horizon, I began to rethink this stranger's story, the kind of story we keep repeating and repeating and repeating, as if the same words are going to change it.

I hoped she still saw the birds.

PETTY

Alaska summer comes on like a drug, bright green and gaudy then forgotten in the cold haze of late September. It's the annual boom to the bust of winter, when most of the jobs, the people who work them, and the tourists who pay for it leave for warmer places where the bar windows aren't boarded up. The Great American Wilderness, untouched, untrammeled, and for four months of the year, like so many tourist destinations, host of a grownup summer camp for people unfit or uninterested in "real jobs." Each generation of seasonal employees thinks they're the first to think of the nicknames: Never-Never Land, the Land of Misfit Toys. Each generation thinks they're the first to switch the *I* to spell "Denial," as in "My summer in Denial." Clichés abound. "What happens in _____ stays in _____," and so on.

Which is to say we take pride in social obliviousness. Which is to say we sometimes feel ourselves exempt. We really might not know any better. Actions are viewed as separate from context, and here, even context is removed from context. Each summer is a new lifetime. Each summer dive bar a testament to the routine of forgetting.

For a few summers, I go out most nights, maybe do a shot with a guy everyone likes and I think I should, too, even though I find his theatrics overwrought, his charisma somewhat lacking. We have what I think is a half-decent conversation, and then later he asks me to kiss him. My suspicions confirmed, but I keep talking. I remind him he's married, which he declares irrelevant and persists. Maybe it is. What do I know. I try to turn the conversation back to work, to the park, to the fluctuating wolf population, but I don't walk away. On the shuttle home, a fifteen-passenger van driven by a sober twenty-three-year-old with a saint's patience for shit-faced old men, he dives over a seat and latches teeth onto my shoulder, through two layers of clothing, and there will be bite marks in the morning. No one is surprised. He has a reputation. He has a great mustache. He is, generally speaking, forgiven. Other women forgive him for worse, or knew better than to engage at all. I'm called petty for holding the grudge.

Another night, same bar, different man. This one can't hold down a job, can't hide his addictions, makes art he can't sell. He has the facial hair and social skills of a man who lives alone all winter without running water or a mirror. I've been warned: he is To Be Avoided. But I feel for him, as I believe humans should feel for each other, wish for him health and comfort in his own skin. I, too, struggle to turn time into money. I, too, feel smarter when I'm drinking. Once, he tells me I'm "the best intellectual we've got," and in the wilderness of Denali/Denial, where one can be a "badass" but rarely an "intellectual," that means something, even coming from him, so I talk. Like adults might. Like I don't know any better. He's read some books. So have I.

He takes conversation as a promise. I say it isn't, that I'm going home with someone else. There's gotta be someone else here, someone sober, or close enough, with a car—there usually is. Even though he promises a good Scrabble game (I'm the best intellectual, after all) and the best head of my life. He turns to leave, then thinks better of it, turns back and kicks my shins, hard, like a tire he wishes weren't flat, and keeps kicking past me and into the wall. If he weren't so clumsy drunk, he'd take me with him, but I am less drunk, mad, and faster, and I am bored with this shit. My legs bruise. I go home alone.

These stories are met with eye rolling, with "oh, that so-and-so, what do you expect." Depending on the perceived charm of the drunk in question, there is an affectionate grin or a disgusted snort. There is no mention of a violent culture of entitlement. There is no mention of the rampant alcoholism in seasonal communities. There are no apologies. That's just what men do when they think no one's watching, when "no one" means a room full of people, half of whom think the place disappears once snow falls. What happens stays. And so on.

I stopped leaving when the bars closed, and then I stopped caring when they reopened in spring. Maybe year-round residence means accountability. Maybe it means you just get used to drinking at home, or you learn to let your grudges walk into the bar before your curiosity. Every good mustache, every man selling jewelry out of his pockets, and every woman giving him the benefit of the doubt starts to look the same, and they frequent every seasonal dive bar.

The Denali biter retired. He's featured on T-shirts, on Adopt-A-Highway road signs, an annual company event named in his honor. A Never-Never-Land legend.

The kicker lost his license and hitchhikes a lot, year-round, bundled thumb out at twenty below, trying to get to town, or the post office.

I used to pick him up, but I don't anymore.

WARRANTY

As a teenager, walking in the Northwood Cemetery in Cambridge, Ohio, I tried to ignore the soccer moms in pink leggings whose hair didn't bounce as they jogged and the kids learning to ride bikes without training wheels. I had a narrow sense of who and what I wanted to see wandering among the headstones and Middle American mortals simply going about their day was not it.

The local paper sometimes referenced generic rumors of a "lady in white" who roamed the grounds crying for a lost child or lover, but she never appeared to me. Despite the absence of anything overtly supernatural or even spooky, the dismal nature of the seasons during which my family tended to visit cultivated my sense of superficial morbidity: leafless ash and buckeye branches against a flat gray winter sky, sometimes spitting snow, everything saturated with cold brown damp. It was easy to imagine a spirit, held in place by too much stone and metal for a year too long, becoming restless and taking drastic action to avoid one more Ohio winter.

But as hard as I tried, I never saw anything like that, and evidence suggested instead a content and sedentary spirit society. The population of Cambridge peaked in the 1930s. Now, the number of buried dead in this cemetery alone is almost double that of those living within the town limits.

In his high school photography class, my dad developed several black-and-white double-exposures of the Cambridge cemetery's main gate framing his own translucent face, a self-portrait hovering in the sky. When I was sixteen, he gave me the Minolta SR-101 camera he'd used thirty years earlier and taught me the word aperture. On a late winter visit to his hometown to visit my grandma, I took the camera and three rolls of black-and-white film to the cemetery, where I finally met someone who was also seeking connection among the graves.

I pointed the camera at a headstone, trying to remember which numbers on the lens referred to focus and which to light, when I heard someone shout, "HEY! Are you a Grateful Dead head?"

I turned to see a pale, round-faced man with a mane of frizzy graying hair and wire-rimmed glasses and in need of a belt. He approached from behind a mausoleum in a waddling gallop.

"Sort of, I guess," I said, which seemed like the closest anyone born in the eighties could hope to be. I understood in that moment that camera-wielding teenagers with cheaply dyed hair wearing odd-fitting sweaters from the thrift store men's rack, too much jewelry, and discount eye makeup were not a common local sight. He recognized in me some shared membership in a subculture of cemetery-haunting wannabe Deadhead loners, and I felt a deep gratitude to my father for leaving Ohio as soon as he was legally able.

"I knew it! Do you want to get high with me behind the mausoleum?"

I did not. I wanted weird romance and enlightenment, but this man had the expectant and slightly confused demeanor of a drugged puppy. I imagined returning stoned to my grandma's house, where she and my immediate family, and maybe some uncles or cousins, would be watching *Jeopardy!* and politely declined. He countered that we could go sit by the creek instead, since the cops came through the cemetery sometimes. I said I needed to go.

"Where do you live?" he asked, and when I said "Arizona," his shoulders slumped. "I should have known you weren't from around here," he said.

My own outsider status may have been evident, though the Watson family has deep roots in south-central Ohio. I knew many of the maiden names of distant cousins and their spinster aunts who rested in these graves, marked mostly by simple granite headstones coated in moss. Other families erected more elaborate memorials: room-sized mausoleums with stained glass windows, engraved benches of reflective marble, carved cherubs or angels who occasionally held American flags. The patriotism disrupted my reveries on death; the ghosts and vampires of my imaginings were primordial and nationless, cared nothing for a lifetime or a year of military service. For a time in the early 1900s, no words were spared on the man's side of the headstone, while the woman's epitaph would read simply, "His wife." Few people leave flowers in these sections, where the most recent deaths occurred in the 1950s. Aesthetically speaking, it's the place to be: none of the gaudiness of the newer plots, where the angels sport pink plastic wings.

I told my new acquaintance that I had relatives buried here but didn't point any of them out. We strolled between the headstones, and I told him I was visiting my grandma. He asked where she lived, maybe he could stop by later, and we could go get a beer. I waved vaguely in a direction away from her house, omitted the fact that I was in high school, and said I had family plans. I left the cemetery in the direction I'd pointed, walking a wide circle, to be sure he wasn't following. This wasn't the romanticized sort of creepy I sought. He annoyed me more than scared me, which annoyed me even more.

He was the only person I ever met in Cambridge who spoke to me when I wasn't with family. I didn't go back to the cemetery on that trip, and by the next, the company of dead strangers—and the living who wandered among them—had lost its appeal.

With the same rootless settlers' mobility afforded my parents, I left Arizona and moved north. The Northwood Cemetery trees continued to grow and shed their leaves, dutifully swept from the pavement and mowed grass. The fracking boom hit Cambridge, which sits on the western edge of the Marcellus Shale formation, and after a few years left vacant hotels, increased assault rates, and just outside the cemetery, a few small oil wells and storage tanks.

The small local oil company's website explains cheerily that directional drilling allows access to oil under "pre-developed" properties, like parks, schools, or cemeteries. Unrestricted by limitations imposed by a vertical line, the possibilities for extraction are endless.

I've stopped a few times at the roadside exhibits along Ohio freeways describing the burial mounds made by people pre-colonization throughout the Midwest and Appalachian Plateau. Referred to by archaeologists as the Adena and Hopewell people, some excavations suggest that they built a small house for a deceased person, then burned it to the ground and covered it in soil. The next burial house would be built on top of the resulting mound. This process of building and burning was repeated, again and again. In the centuries that followed, settlers forcibly displaced the descendants of the mound builders, as well as people from other lineages who had more recently arrived, making way for European farmers like my own ancestors to stake claim to the land. The mounds are now visible from freeways, or in some cases, built over and marked with a sign, evidence of the millennia of living and dying in what is now Ohio, the living world twisting around the burned, overgrown, and violently erased worlds of the dead.

Grandma used to plant marigolds at the base of her husband's headstone, "to keep the ants away," she said. I never asked what ants would have wanted with the grave of a man buried decades ago or why we should be bothered by them, but who doesn't like marigolds, a splash of fire against the granite. Between her name and year of birth and my grandfather's, marked by birth and death, an outline of a generic tree adorns the simple stone. The tree was my grandfather's logo for his hobby woodworking shop, and Grandma said, simply, "I love trees."

As an adult, I visited infrequently, and in those rare summer evenings I'd go with her to water the marigolds. She straightened the small American flags planted loosely at the stone's corner, left on holidays by veterans' organizations, then cleared when deemed too tattered or unseasonable by groundskeepers. My grandfather had gone out for a walk in 1984, soon after I was born, and for years his widow couldn't drive past the corner where his heart failed him. And then, eventually, she could. Their courtship had coincided with the start of the Second World War. The letters they wrote while he flew bombers over Europe and she learned to type underscore nothing to me so much as their youth when they were plunged into their nation's mess of love and war. He returned, and they raised four children in the town where they'd both live all but one year of their lives. She went on without him when he died. She had her belief in heaven as comfort and marigolds as defense.

One night, during the last of my visits when she still kept up the ritual of visiting the cemetery, she seemed to tire of the whole routine and walked on legs bent uncomfortably inward at the knees back to the car, leaving me with the watering can. I watched the water bounce off the orange petals and onto the soil and meticulously groomed grass. I closed my eyes against a wave of vertigo as I pictured the trickle of water and wet earth pressing against whatever remained of my grandfather's long-vacated body, or, more likely, the costly box built to house it. I thought of the myth that hair keeps growing after death. I thought of the drowned squirrel flung from my rain barrel at home and how the following spring all that remained was the skull and a flattened mat of fur.

I imagined roots and earthworms, layers of soil and fire and oil drills now snaking underneath it all. It was all so monumental and mundane, these ways of living and dying on the surface of the earth.

Grandma drove herself home; at eighty-six, she still could. I walked back to her apartment, the smaller, more manageable space she'd recently moved to, on the trail through the cemetery's newest section, where three people sat on plastic benches next to two brown rectangles in the grass. On the next evening's walk I read the markers, which stated that both were recent deaths, people in their twenties. Grave kitsch surrounded them: pastel teddy bears, plastic hearts with rhyming Hallmark poems printed in the center. The mourners each held giant sodas and to my stranger's eyes looked bored to tears.

One evening, after watering the marigolds, I stayed up late, looking through a closet piled with boxes of photo albums, old *Life* magazines, and Grandma's grade school work. My great-step-grandmother, Blanche, died in 1981, and tucked into the guestbook from her funeral, I found an envelope containing one neatly creased sheet of paper: a fifty-year warranty for her casket.

The warranty states that, "upon notice of it, Batesville Casket Company will within ten days replace this casket if, at any time within fifty years after the date of internment, it has failed in any way to resist the entrance of air, water or any element found in the soil in which it was interred." I read and reread. Had it occurred to any of us to check?

Blanche was buried only a few years before my grandfather, whose grave is guarded by marigolds. Her remains occupy the third space marked by a single long, low headstone in the old section of the cemetery. She shares the stone with her husband and his first wife, who died of tuberculosis in 1933. My great-grandfather married Blanche soon after. Grandma told me that her new stepmother discouraged her from keeping a photo of her late mother next to her bed, and I have often wondered if this kind of earthly jealousy was taken into account when buying the three-way headstone.

Using the weak internet signal from the nearby school, I turned to Google, and learned that casket warranties went out of style in the eighties. One man in Minnesota started an online campaign against Batesville, the warranty-issuing casket company, after the casket of a relative, interred above ground and guaranteed for seventy-five years, started leaking "a slimy, smelly stew." He invited other buyers of these caskets to join him in a class action lawsuit.

I thought of the marigolds. Was my grandfather's casket guaranteed against the elements too? How would anyone know if a trickle of water slipped past the roots and into a thirty-year-old vacuum-sealed lid? I hoped just a little bit of water could enter, and a few microbes and bacteria with it, ensuring that time is allowed to pass in a sufficiently oxygenated way. I no longer dreamed of the roaming undead but wished for them a dignified, invisible decomposition, unfettered by the WASPy inventions of pre-engraved headstones and caskets sealed against the biological progression of time.

Joking on the phone with my dad days later, I asked if he wanted to take this to court, and he snorted at the idea and said he just wants to be thrown to the coyotes when he dies. I mentioned contamination of municipal water supplies by decaying bodies, which, in my late night Googling at Grandma's, I learned is a major factor in sealed burials, a practical concern that, like many other factors, I hadn't considered till now. He said something dismissive and, like any good southwestern hypocrite, referenced Edward Abbey: an unmarked grave, a death unencumbered by bureaucracy.

I said, "It's a damn good thing you left Ohio."

He and I have this in common: leaving places behind and revisiting them later, baffled by our own relationships to what has or hasn't changed in our absence. To the trite absurdity of learning relatives' names on headstones and pointing as if at distant birds: *Look, there's one of us,* and walking past. We all move on. We are all forgotten. There will be no one to water the marigolds, and nothing to water.

As Ohio warms, rain falls heavier and longer, with hotter, drier days in between. It's getting harder to grow anything reliably.

I had the outline of my grandfather's tree logo tattooed on my back. The artist asked what kind of tree it's supposed to be, and I said I didn't know and realized that not knowing was almost part of the point. Maybe an elm. Maybe 1950s clip art. Maybe a tenuous grasp to form a lasting bond with a place and a lineage I could easily forget if it were not drawn onto my body.

I'd told Grandma I planned on getting the tattoo. She'd struggled when my aunt had a floral design tattooed on her ankle and with my first meaningless doodles at eighteen but in her final years, she saved her judgments for the consequential. "That makes sense," she said, which was something like a blessing.

A year later, I was unable to travel to Ohio for her funeral. The family who was able to and selected local friends gathered, masked and distanced, and I watched a recording of the service later. My dad and his brothers each spoke. My mom texted me pictures from the funeral home. Later, she sent pictures of my cousins carrying the casket to a graveside platform covered inexplicably in Astroturf, protected from the rain by a popup tent. Chairs around the grave were draped in blue faux velvet that reminded me, viscerally, of a Cookie Monster costume I wore for a middle school event. My cousins' kids, masks down, posed under umbrellas for photos.

Grandma had been ready to go. There was no tragedy in her death, and the year, 2020, would be carved into the headstone later. Thousands of miles away, I knew with certainty that I would never get high behind the mausoleum.

I would never know what kind of tree is drawn on my back, out of sight. In clearing out the final boxes from Grandma's closet, my parents found Blanche's casket warranty and sent it to me. "We know you were interested in this," they said. The fifty-year mark approaches fast.

On my last visit, a year and a half before Grandma's death, my dad and I met in Cambridge. The three of us spent slow days together, and as always, my dad was recognized in the grocery store and sparsely attended church as a good son, a son who left but always came back, and I was introduced, again, as the "granddaughter from Alaska" to faint nods and smiles and sometimes a comment about reality TV I'd never seen. It was May, and Grandma said it got too hot to sit on the porch swing earlier in the day than it ever used to, so she napped. We ordered pizza. After she was in bed, Dad and I drank beers on the porch, talking about his childhood. I woke early to walk or run in the cemetery before the heat. Some mornings mist hung over the creek, muting the green of the trees. It was not a mist I could imagine anyone mistaking for a ghost.

Heavy equipment downed trees and leveled out the remaining hills alongside the path for a cemetery expansion. Not a lot of open space remained between the existing burials and the road.

The fenced-in oil well along the path between the cemetery and Grandma's apartment pumped diligently, smelling like hot oil as the sun climbed higher.

This is not reported as a haunting either.

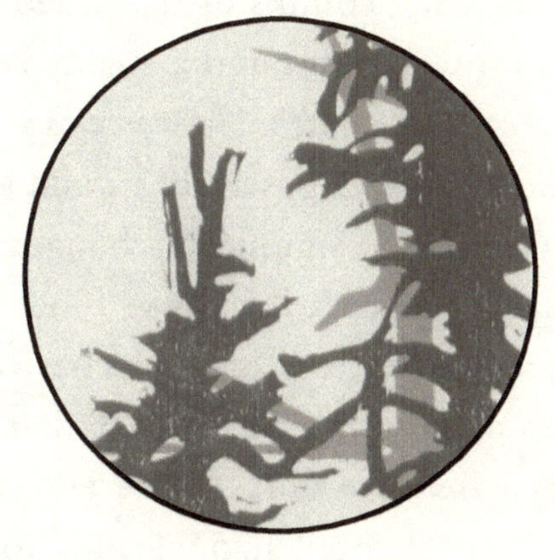

SHORELINE

1. Six to Ten Places to Visit before They're Gone

In 2006, I spent an entire day on a crowded observation deck watching Patagonia's largest advancing glacier, Perito Moreno, calve into the water. At the time, the glacier was described as "defiant" for its continued growth in a warming world, as if ice melts due to weakness of character.

I was young and cheap and didn't want to pay for the boat ride around Lago Argentina, its bright blue surface scattered with floating chunks of discarded ice, so I was limited to one vantage point and a steady soundtrack of multilinguistic tourist chatter. It was quite boring after a while: too much time to passively sit and stare and too little time to witness any significant changes in global climate patterns. I thought a lot about food during those hours. But there was only one daily bus between the town and the glacier, and I reminded myself that there might not be glaciers when I'm old. At one end of the observation deck, a hand-painted sign warning tourists not to climb the railing depicted an image of an ice projectile impaling a startled stick figure's head. So I stayed on the deck, watching, hour after hour, trying to focus on the privilege of sharing the world with ice rather than fantasizing about what I'd eat when I got back to town.

Perito Moreno rose more than fifty meters above the surface of the water, and the sign marked the distance as fourteen kilometers between the glacier's toe and the visible base of the mountains, seven- to nine-thousand-foot peaks named after explorers with European names. As time passed, the sky filled with thin, high clouds, dulling the blue light reflected off the ice. I fell asleep on a bench.

It's a strange kind of conquest, travel motivated by the anticipation of loss, a sort of prelude to nostalgia. On the regularly published lists of six to ten places to visit before climate change destroys them, there was always at least one glacial site; even before climate dominated headlines, ice was unanimously recognized as endangered. An obvious criticism of these lists is that increased air or cruise ship travel only adds to the problem, but the lists aren't claiming to solve anything, and our emotional response to climate change is about more than science and accusations of hypocrisy. There's another impulse at work here, a desire to establish a connection because loss is imminent but not before.

Is this a consequence of having too much information or of being mortal?

2. Summer Flooding

Later the same year, at the northern end of the chain of mountain ranges tracing the western edge of the Americas, I thought I was falling in love with someone who was dying. I wouldn't have done it if I'd known he'd live. We both knew it was a bad idea from the start, a betrayal of friendships and loyalties. I pursued it anyway because the diagnosis left him six months, a year at most, and I calculated that opportunity outweighed good judgment. I was young. He wasn't old, but maybe illness made him feel like he was. I was driven by an urgency, a fear of loss, of missing something I would live to regret missing.

The inevitable ending shaped the affection between us. I claimed powerlessness in the face of it, because to do otherwise would be to claim responsibility. I remember clearly how intense each moment felt in the wake of that reality that turned out not to be. His illness made walking long distances difficult, and on hikes together, I slowed my usually quick pace to his. I assigned great importance to our frequent stops, taking the chance to observe my surroundings, feel the wind, more fully absorb each moment. I tried to explain this to him, and he sarcastically thanked me for finding such joy in his limitations. I learned more birdcalls that summer than any summer since. A day hike up a mountain felt like a negotiation with death. Splitting a bagel at the summit was a sacrament.

He had a complicated, risk-laden surgery scheduled for midwinter, and we parted ways at the end of August. I had an evening flight out of Anchorage and an 11 a.m. class the next day in Tucson, but a flooded creek closed the one road that could get me there. It had been raining nonstop for days, and snowing in the mountains. Unable to leave, we had breakfast. I poked at my eggs, watched the water pour off the roof of the café in steady sheets, hypnotized by how quickly water in an unexpected place can change the course of a day, or a life. I considered dropping out of college, getting married, going back to bed; the flooded creek was a sign that plans should change. I was always looking for signs then, something to absolve me of choice. But after two phone calls, I had a connecting flight from Fairbanks, and that was that. The power of water mitigated by efficient customer service.

Over the following year, I learned that I was wrong on at least two counts: what we shared was not love, and he did not die. Now, years later, he is still alive and well.

Sometimes, modern medicine is both flawed in its assessment and miraculous in its treatments. The surgery was successful. By the time it became clear that he would not die, at least not soon and of the assumed illness, he stopped calling, and eventually, I did too. We each did things we'd once said we'd never do: he got married, and I bought a car. Our attentions can be so short-lived. Fear of loss removed, what felt like love came into focus as only distraction.

3. Bibliography

In his 2004 book about Arctic climate science, *The Whale and the Supercomputer: On the Northern Front of Climate Change*, journalist Charles Wohlforth wrote, "The climate we perceive is a metaphor for the sum of weather conditions over a chosen span of time and space. Knowing an area's climate is like knowing a person: the sense of a personality develops through observation until it seems solid and tangible, but that sense is never more than an estimation and often has to be adjusted to account for new events. A climate exists only in the context of sufficiently broad boundaries, and boundaries must be chosen one way or another."

Sometimes I wonder what it would be like to get to know a place, a ridgeline, a river, or a weather pattern, and not immediately think of what threatens it. This would likely be an exercise in compressing the boundaries of time and space, as Wohlforth suggests, down to only the intimately tangible and experienced: the crunch-crunch of boots on dry, packed snow or melting the ring of ice from a lover's eyelashes, or your own, with a briefly ungloved finger.

I am not native to northern cold but came to it by choice, and I'm learning about this kind of cold as it is pushed from the planet.

I learned after a few years that as winter settles in, my body fights it. I overdress, trying to shield my skin from any contact with the air. My muscles tense, and I walk too fast, eyes down, fingers clenched into fists. I take shallow breaths, as if the cold will crack something inside. I cry easily and try to limit my time outside.

Each year after about three weeks of struggle against the season, there is a distinct moment when I accept it, welcome it, allow myself to breathe again. It always happens at night, usually in late October, but now, sometimes much later in the season. I'll uncover my face, let the cold touch me, allow it to dictate the pace of my movements. I don't want to lose the peace this moment always brings, the feeling of being present in the world, even at what can feel like its most unwelcoming season.

The earth's tilt guarantees that winter in the north will always be cold, which provides some comfort in the face of all the frantic warnings, but the specifics are more nebulous. The few years I used to base my assessment of "normal" are abnormalities. I've learned that spring used to come slower, and later, and that what I call a "cold snap" wasn't always considered long enough or cold enough to warrant that name.

Annie Dillard wondered "how long would you have to live on earth before you could feel with any assurance that any one particular long period of cold would, in fact, end?" She assumed, as any reasonable temperate dweller might, that warmth is the desired state and that one would want it to end.

I read Dillard around the same time I first encountered Inuit environmental leader Sheila Watts-Cloutier's use of the phrase "the right to be cold" in framing advocacy for climate action as a human rights issue not only for Arctic Indigenous people but also, as she'd later write in her memoir by the same title, "as a gift from Inuit hunters and elders . . . to a culture that had largely lost its sense of place and position in the natural world." I also started to notice bumper stickers plastered mostly on very large pickups bearing the slogan "Alaskans for global warming," another way of saying that warmth was preferred over cold regardless of geography. In conversation with "the right to be cold," the sticker read as an aggression, aligned with the violence of colonialism. Most people in my life, meanwhile, spoke of climate change at some distance, mostly in terms of data sets, rather than rights or desire: glacial ice lost, tenths of degrees Celsius warmed, future studies planned, a vague sense of unease about what might happen next. Sometimes I wonder what might be different if more scientists had recognized sooner the necessity of integrating the human story into the scientific one, if the gift of Indigenous climate knowledge had been received sooner and more gracefully.

Everyone brings to their present lives a certain set of assumptions and norms, and desire springs from them. I discovered that the patterns I learned are not necessarily patterns at all. This is what is happening right now, I told myself, because it is all I can really know for sure. Breathe the cold in. Don't fight it. Don't try to hold it. Knowledge has always been tenuous.

4. A Chosen Span of Time and Space

I know this for sure: the changeability of both bodies and water makes me nervous.

Craig and I fell in love over a wet, cool subarctic summer, to the steady sound of rain on the roof. Had those months been warmer, we might have spent more time outside, but given the circumstances, we chose sheltered warmth and a lot of time holed up in bed. In choosing to stay with him through the winter and the winters to follow, I chose also the cold, the dark, the frosty eyelashes and endangered landscapes of the North. I chose to stay in the land of ascending tree line, eroding coastlines, and politics often dominated by those who have, as Watts-Cloutier writes, "lost their sense of place in the natural world" and appear uninterested in finding it.

In staying, I chose to accept the responsibility and fear for another's bodily well-being that intimacy creates and the knowledge that, given the numerical data, he will likely die before me. I've accepted the kind of fear that keeps people who are prone to panic about the far-off inevitable awake at night.

Maybe I invent these moments of crisis to make up for the lack of them in the life and routines we share. Sometimes I miss the dramas of my life before him, and the only thing I can think to pit us against is abstractly impending death. "Maybe life is like a river," he suggested once, unoriginal but well meaning. The river's biography tells of a raging and fast-moving current at its source, slowing into canyons and meanders, and eventually leveling into the watershed's terminus.

But what it means to be "like a river" is changing too. So many rivers no longer reach the sea. I pointed this out, never knowing when to let a metaphor die. And metaphors of love and water abound.

Zora Neale Hurston's character Janie, in the classic novel *Their Eyes Were Watching God*, says, "Love is like the sea. It's a moving thing, but still and all, it takes its shape from the shore it meets, and it's different with every shore." In this novel, and in today's shifting climate, too much water in the wrong place at the wrong time changes lives. The sea is rising. What has not been a shore before is becoming one. I don't think this makes Janie's statement about the nature of love any less true, but it certainly shifts the boundaries.

In a colder time, the water that now forms the northern Bering and Chukchi Seas formed ice fields across much of North America, and what is now covered by water between Alaska and Siberia was dry land. I've known this history for years, but it awed me to learn that there are still underwater riverbeds carved into what was once the subcontinent of Beringia. The earth has many kinds of memory.

I don't want to be driven by fear of loss, but I do want to remember. I want to remember the sound of glacial calving, the rapid, jerky sway of an alpine flower in the wind, my love's hands in mine, both of ours made cold by the northern air. Ice will melt, these tundra ecologies may top out and be gone, like us. I don't want to embrace them only because they'll disappear, but because, for now, they are here, and so am I. And some memory of all this will still exist, like riverbeds under the sea. Like a half-shed tear freezing and thawing and freezing again with each blink of a watchful eye.

CULTIVATION

Lettuce

Before I'd started keeping clean socks and underwear and a box of my favorite teas at Craig's house, I called him from a grocery store seed display in Fairbanks. I explained with dispassionate reason why I wanted to resurrect a corner—just one corner—of the greenhouse on his property, which had lain dormant since his ex-wife left years before.

"Just some lettuce and maybe a few herbs," I said, staring at the pictures of shiny vegetables glittering under fluorescent lights. Possibility radiated from the packages. I wanted to lick them. "I swear I'm not gonna try to move in or anything." It hadn't yet occurred to me that one day I might want to.

He readily agreed. We brought out in each other this ready agreement, this openness to possibility. We weren't yet ready to name it, only to quietly nurture it and see what would grow. Still, we viewed our romance as a temporary thing, an impractical but comfortable resting place on the way to whatever came next. And in the meantime, we needed to eat, and we both enjoyed fresh greens.

The greenhouse is barn shaped, built by the previous owners in the early 1980s of now cold-cracked and sunbaked fiberglass panels and a scrap-wood frame. Two narrow raised beds ran the length of it, and a box built onto a four-by-eight-foot sheet of plywood sat on rotting pallets in the center.

The soil hadn't been turned in years. When I first dug in, I found, to my horror and confusion, Styrofoam packing peanuts embedded throughout. I didn't know much about gardening, but growing food in petrochemicals offended my vision of what it should entail. I started to pick them out by hand, one by one. Craig laughed, said his ex had tried the same thing and had given up around 1997. The previous owners had mixed them in with the soil for aeration and filler, and once I'd removed enough of them I started to see why. They were more easily available than specialty garden products, especially thirty years earlier, and the soil was dense and compacted without them. I realized that the growing season was too short to worry about purity and resigned myself to the pellets, only picking them out when they appeared on the surface.

Everything grows from what came before. Sometimes the messiest choices are the ones that let us bloom.

Kale

At first, I wanted only to grow what was easy and threw a handful of kale seeds in the center bed. As seed leaves the size of pinheads emerged and spring grew into summer, I obsessed on the plants' rapid growth. Craig decided that the greenhouse doorframe was too old and rotten to withstand the number of times I was opening and closing it and replaced the hinges and wood with newer scraps. Still, it was low-consequence renovation, a project from which either of us could walk away at any time. We were cautious but fascinated by the way a seed could sprout into food, and each repair and upgrade was a way of investing in its success.

The kale thrived and grew into thick-stalked purple-green shrubs with leaves the size of my torso. By solstice, the diet for our unofficially combined household evolved around ways to work these rich greens into every meal.

Radish

"Think of a radish," my friends printed on T-shirts in college, a pun on the shared etymology of the words *root,* as in the part of a plant that grows in the ground, radical, pertaining to roots and thus to the origin of everything, to the extremities, and evolving to mean unconventional or far from the mainstream, and *radish,* a root vegetable whose name derives from the same Latin origin. We were all looking for ways to be recognized then: as radicals, as free from convention, as reaching for something other than the obvious.

Political organizer Saul Alinsky wrote in 1971 that while there are no rules for revolution, there are "rules for radicals who want to change their world," countering the notion that living and working in or striving for the extremities, politically or otherwise, is done without structure or strategy. I took it to heart when a Swiss German neighbor asked about my planting schedule, and when I said I didn't have anything in the greenhouse yet, followed up with characteristic directness, easily misunderstood as judgment, "Why would you not have radishes planted by April 15?" It seemed too early, the ground often snow-covered, but she'd been at this longer than I, and I adjusted my schedule to meet hers. In the coming years, I learned that radishes function as a signal: it can take days or weeks for the soil to warm up enough for germination, but once they do, they tell the gardener that the soil is ready for other seeds.

If one root is growing, there will be more.

Tomato

Word got out that Craig and I were gardening together. A neighbor who takes his vegetables seriously invited us over for coffee. We left his house hours later with several broccoli and tomato starts and a Ziploc bag full of his old seeds. We took the gift as approval. People ask about your tomato plants in a way they don't ask about your sex life: Are you watering every day? Are you watching for bugs? You shouldn't ever need to hand-pollinate if you have your timing right. Timing, really, is everything.

It was sheer luck, but my first tomatoes grew easy. Even half-ignored and un-pruned, the cherry varieties our neighbor gave us spilled their long vines out of their pots, red eclipsing green on sun-ripened fruits in late July, like magic. I felt like I'd achieved a dream I didn't know I had: to feed a man with an endless supply of a very specific kind of homegrown salad.

Still, most years, regardless of my tweaks in planting dates or variables in spring warmth, plenty of green tomatoes still hang on the vines when nights begin to freeze in the fall. Nothing can be done to adjust the earth's tilt away from the sun. I learned to be more ruthless in cutting my losses, cutting the vines from the roots to hang inside, but still, most Septembers, the massive plants crowd inside against the south-facing window. They seem ridiculously vulnerable and out of place against the first snow. They block the diminishing light through the window. They drop a mess of yellowing leaves that crunch underfoot, and ripe fruit plunks to the floor if we brush against the vines in passing. We step on dropped tomatoes in socked feet in the new dark, and track their goo around the house. The last tomatoes are envoys from one season into the next, and when they're gone, we reclaim the house, vacuum the soil and crinkled leaves from the floor, and settle into the dark months together, fulfillment of another dream I didn't know I had.

Broccoli

I learned about seed starting calendars and started taking notes on planting and germination dates. They crept earlier and earlier in the season every year, past what could reasonably be called spring, when the ground was still unquestionably snow-covered and the rivers frozen solid but the sun climbing high enough in the sky to produce warmth you don't have to imagine, and into what can really only be accurately called winter.

My friend Sarah's baby was born in February, and the first time she brought him over, my broccoli seeds had just sprouted in the windowsill. As I held the baby, his eyes opening and closing as he squirmed in my arms, I realized that I'd planted my first round of seeds the day he was born. Now both life forms, wobbly and unstable but gaining strength daily, sat in my living room.

"Can I take a picture of him with a seedling?" I asked suddenly, and Sarah, a botanist, said, "Of course." I propped up the baby, now fussing and red-faced, with pillows on the couch and next to him a four-inch-tall broccoli plant in a plastic pot and snapped a photo. We kept it up through the spring and summer, as his fingers learned to grab the broccoli leaves and pull, and the stem grew strong enough to withstand it. He gnawed on the leaves through the summer, the massive plant swallowing him, and that fall, he could eat some of the blanched stems.

We kept it up for several years, tracking his growth alongside a new broccoli plant. The baby grew and learned to help transplant his broccoli into the greenhouse in the spring and to harvest it in the fall.

After his second birthday and the germination of that year's broccoli but long before the snow melted, he and Sarah waited while I dressed to leave the house and join them on a ski. I rotated the seedlings in the windowsill so they wouldn't lean too far in only one direction to reach the light, and switched on two table fans so the plants could "exercise" while I was out, mimicking the wind they'd experience if they'd been planted in a place where they wouldn't die outside before mid-May.

Sarah watched from the doorway, her son's head peeking over her shoulder, noting my attention to water, wind, and light. "What would it be like, I wonder, if we paid as much attention to native plants as we do to our gardens," she mused. She spent her summers crawling and bushwhacking through marshy buggy bogs in search of mosses and lichens, whose growing conditions might vary in such a small and particular way as to produce a distinct variety. Paying attention to their needs would mean being tuned into changes in temperature, moisture, light, or nitrogen and adjusting our behaviors when we noted the changes occurring.

I left the fan on low, the leggy seedlings swaying in artificial wind. Outside, snow would keep falling for another month or two, temperatures mostly well below freezing, the mosses and lichens buried in snow.

Beans

I grew up with a vegetable garden but never considered it mine. My mom grew greens, radishes, beans, and squash in every place we lived, in containers or small ground plots. In many of those places, heat and drought were the limiting factors rather than rapidly changing sunlight and the ubiquitous threat of frost that shapes Alaska gardens. But she valued the process of knowing what it took to keep a seed alive and made the time to care for them as they grew.

Her care for plants includes wild and cultivated, indoor and outdoor. When she lived in the Upper Peninsula of Michigan, she wrote an indoor horticulture column for the *Grand Marais Pilot*, the small local paper, and explained her short absence from the column and neglect of her houseplants and dog because a demanding newcomer had arrived in her house: me. "I can look up the jade plant, find out how much light and how much water it needs, the flowers it may produce under maximum conditions, and how to propagate it," she wrote. "Millions of jades exist, all requiring the same treatment, all behaving similarly when conditions are altered. There are countless baby humans too, and lots of books about how to care for them." But each baby is unique, she explained;

you can't look up your own baby in Dr. Spock. So she was left wondering if the conditions she was providing would have the desired outcome, and she wouldn't know for years. The jade plant, at least, could communicate by thriving or dying.

We left the Upper Peninsula soon after. The houseplants crossed state lines, some lived, some died. In Flagstaff, years later, she had the space for a backyard garden again.

In the horticulture column that was actually about me, she wondered if I'd be "dull and bored with life" as a teenager. I wasn't that exactly, but I wasn't flowering either. I was a good student, loved school, and wanted to do well, but in middle school that became a struggle rather than a joy. My mom saw my despondent attitude about going to school one day and informed me that I would be staying home with her and planting beans. The teacher whose workload contributed the most to my anxiety made it clear she disapproved—her students were "supposed to be stressed" by the challenges of gifted education, she said—but my mom stuck with her decision.

She poked small holes in mounds of soil, and I glumly followed her down the row, dropping a bean in each hole, covering it, and patting it down. She says after a row, I was starting to speak again, and by the time we finished planting, I had smiled. It didn't fix everything, but it helped. My mom still tells this as a story of the healing power of gardening, which science has supported again and again.

Decades later, I talked about our middle school experience with a classmate who graduated valedictorian and became a medical doctor. "I wish someone had taught me how to grow beans instead of that class. Then at least I'd have some beans," she said.

Sometimes, when we don't know what to talk about, we talk about plants: which houseplant cuttings are doing well, which have turned yellow and dropped leaves, how garden planning, planting, or harvesting is going. We rarely talk about the mind and body's need for soil in our fingernails, about the darkness made a bit gentler by a seed pressed into earth, and the days waiting for its first push into the promise of light.

Rutabaga

Pasties are a staple of Upper Peninsula cuisine. In their most unadulterated form, which is what my parents were introduced to at community events and school fundraisers in their few years living there, they consist only of minimally seasoned ground meat, potatoes, and rutabaga—a root vegetable closely related to and sometimes synonymous with a turnip—baked into a handheld pastry. They're an aggressively unfussy food, meant to be packed and carried and to last a person through a long and tiring day. Pasties' cultural origins are traced to regions known for bland flavors and grueling work ethics, and their ingredients traced to short growing seasons and early winters. I grew up hearing more amused references to my parents' days in the land of pasties than eating them.

The rutabaga also appears in improvisational composer Frank Zappa's 1967 song "Call Any Vegetable," a genre-defying musical assurance that a vegetable will respond when called. In the libretto that accompanied the album, *Absolutely Free,* Zappa wrote of the song's meaning, "People who do not live up to their responsibilities are vegetables. I feel that these people, even if they are inactive, apathetic or unconcerned at this point, can be motivated toward a more useful sort of existence. I believe that if you call any vegetable it will respond to you." The song's interlude departs from the orchestral rock arrangements that defined Zappa's music in a brief vocal solo, a tuneless crooning of one vegetable's name: Ruta-bay-ay-ayga.

My dad may have listened to Zappa more often when he had the house to himself, opting out of explaining the text and subtext of political, sexual, and social satire over and over again to two young children, but he'd play the "rutabaga song" on request, and we'd all join in a living room chorus: CALL ANY VEGETABLE, CALL IT BY NAME.

I chose the rutabaga as the subject of a middle school assignment to give a short speech on what food you would be, citing reasons such as my Yooper origins and my relative obscurity, and a proposition that while I may be an acquired taste, I was actually very adaptable and added value to a variety of situations. I'm not sure I'd knowingly eaten a rutabaga at that point, and I was painfully shy among my peers, so while the composition came as no challenge, I recall the delivery as a tortuous endeavor, likely for my teacher and classmates as well as me.

Zappa wrote in *Absolutely Free* that he and his band, the Mothers of Invention, wanted to reach the people "on the *fringe* of everything . . . those few who have the power within themselves to cause or motivate social change but have never used it for one reason or another."

Rutabaga grows well in the Interior, and if you get the timing right, they can be ready for harvest by early July. I like to marinate them in oil and herbs for an easy contribution to the grill for potluck dinners. Countless times, I have arrived at a gathering and suddenly forgotten conversational conventions, and at a loss for anything to say, ask anyone in earshot, "So, you all know Frank Zappa's song about the rutabaga, right?"

They rarely do.

Almanac

For a time, whenever she called from Southern California, Craig's mother, Ruth, would ask what we were growing in the garden. The answer was the same from week to week: lettuce, kale, tomatoes, broccoli, beans, carrots, peas, chard. It was growing well, and yes, we ate a lot of salad in the summer, so nice to hear from you, so sorry, I've got to get going, talk to you soon, yes, C-H-A-R-D, it's another leafy green.

Maybe we were impatient with the meandering, repetitive conversation and felt like she was inventing ways to keep us on the phone longer than we wanted. The long summer days were fleeting, and there is always a long list of things that need doing. But that September, Craig got word that she had fallen, and the care facility would not discharge her without someone to sign her out. She was diagnosed with dementia and was no longer able to live alone, as she had for decades in the same house where Craig grew up.

He flew south, and I soon followed, after a few more days spent putting the garden to sleep for the winter. I arrived with the Santa Ana winds, which broke branches from trees overnight, and hot days that made the work of sorting through decades of clutter and deep cleaning a long-lived-in house difficult.

But she had always been a chronicler, and every crevasse was tucked with notebooks, photo albums, and scraps of paper scribbled with lists. I felt like an interloper, categorizing the papers into keep or toss piles, but Craig and his brother were occupied with their own childhoods, finances, senior care facilities in Oregon, where his brother lived, finding a real estate agent. Sometimes I'd ask Ruth about something I found, whether she'd like to keep it. "Why are we doing this?" she asked me, which was a harder question to answer than the one I'd expected: "Who are you and why are you in my house?"

In her final cognizant years, Ruth had joined a seniors' writing group at the Pico Rivera community center and had filled two bookshelves with three-ring binders containing typed accounts of her own memories, second-hand tellings of events in her sons' lives, and occasionally, biting social commentary. We invited members of her group over to take things of hers they wanted: end tables, casserole dishes, jewelry. When several of them arrived together, I referred to them as "the writers," and one of the men, white ponytailed with white socks pulled to his knees, turned to me with unexpected defensiveness and said, "We are not writers. We are just people who want to remember things."

When the people who want to remember things left, we went back to cleaning. On Ruth's desk, I found multiple lists labeled "Craig and Erica's garden," transcriptions of what we'd said over the phone: kale, tomatoes, broccoli, lettuce, beans, chard, peas, carrots. We hadn't recognized what was happening.

In *The Faraway Nearby*, Rebecca Solnit writes about her mother's dementia alongside studies of Arctic ice. "Nothing decays in extreme cold. . . . Cold preserves almost anything," she notes. "The very word *freeze* is synonymous in modern English with stopping time, stopping progress, stopping a film, and if time is a river, then perhaps its water may turn to ice." In contrast to the way dementia melts holes in the brain, deep cold serves as ecological memory. But this memory, too, is threatened by warming.

I struggled to abandon Ruth's notes, which weren't limited to our garden, but to so many other observations and reminders signaling that she, in her solitude, knew that a part of herself was melting. I kept a few of her papers, but we were rushed by sudden and unanticipated timelines: the realtor wanted to paint the kitchen before listing the house, Craig's brother needed to get back to Oregon, and it was so, so hot—forgetting weather—and we were tired, and it was trash day, so most of her lists and notes were discarded, forgotten.

Except for this: I am just a person, trying to remember things. Kale, tomatoes, broccoli, lettuce, beans, chard, peas, carrots.

Corn

I've learned that they may not thrive, but most seeds will grow where they're planted, even if conditions are far from ideal.

Compost

Everything dies in the end.

I built my first compost box of old plywood and shipping pallets, haphazardly screwed together, then built a second one, and then integrated a plastic tub where broken down stems and food scraps are sifted through wire mesh and wait till the next planting season. Compost is a slow process at high latitude: the decaying pile is frozen half the year, and it accumulates faster than it breaks down.

One summer when I worked guiding hikes, I met a kid from New Jersey who'd won his trip to Alaska for himself and his family for outstanding performance in a national science fair competition. His project was to design and implement composting at a municipal level. I described the challenges of composting in the subarctic mountains:

long winters, deep cold, inconsistent summer rains. He was unimpressed with my excuses. "You just need more," he insisted. "It doesn't matter how cold it gets. You could have a pile as big as a house, and it'll cook all year."

He wasn't wrong. I learned that three cubic feet, properly mixed, can stay thawed, even actively breaking down, or "cooking," in the center regardless of air temperature. It's easy to maintain the volume, but harder to keep an ideal combination of moisture and matter. Still, I think of that kid every time I drive a pitchfork down into a rock-hard mound of months-old coffee grounds, during my absurd January attempts to expedite gardening season by sheer force of will. The extra minutes of sunlight after winter solstice spark a hopeless fever for bare hands in soil, months too soon.

Table scraps and dried peavines of years past become the soil for the next. I began as a purist but gradually learned to add spoiled milk, chicken bones, fish carcasses, a wool sock worn beyond repair, anything that eventually decays with time. One year, I mixed twenty salmon heads and carcasses with sawdust and water in five-gallon buckets in an effort to make my own fertilizer, and the stench of rot lingered on everything the bubbling concoction touched even through the frozen months. While I attempted to strain the solids from the liquids, magpies dropped by to check out the smell but opted to leave it alone, too much death even for their scavenging palettes. It was one of the most disgusting things I've ever done, but it made the plants grow bigger.

Composting is a commitment to stay and see a cycle through to some sort of completion, though the end is never clear. The garden will sprout and grow and flourish in a few months, its rewards tangible and edible and gone, but rot, decay, and rebirth takes years. And I am here for it, again and again.

All right then, let me try to rephrase.
When I was alive, I aimed to be a student
not of longing but of light.

—Maggie Nelson
Bluets

COLOR-CODED AND ABRIDGED FIELD NOTES ON THE END OF THE WORLD

Last hands to touch the peel

Much of the year, the nonhuman world appears in a dichromatic scale: white snow, spruce black against snow and sky, shadow shades of gray or hints of blue. We leave our colorful little human things scattered on trails and around our houses.

Hunter's orange camouflages with the explosion of color in the tundra in the fall, the season it's intended for, but in the winter landscape orange stands out to me as the most human: plastic sleds pulled behind skiers, Arctic oven tents, reflective stripes on gear and machinery, or orange peels dropped in snow, their frozen slices eaten from gloved fingers.

Once, driving to Fairbanks on a spring morning, I followed a trail of what looked like a case worth of those easy orange peels, dotting the recently melted out highway centerline for miles. I imagined a solitary driver, window open on this first truly warm morning of the season, peeling fruit after fruit, some one-handed, the peel flung out the window whole, others a more frustrated effort, maybe a slight swerve into the wrong lane as both hands came into play, smaller pieces tossed out like breadcrumbs. It went on like this for forty miles. It started to seem excessive. I couldn't make sense of the scale. Unless maybe the orange peeler was feeding a busload of children. Maybe they feared scurvy. I felt some relief when it ended.

What I'm describing aren't standard oranges, but Cuties, the specifically bred and marketed mini-fruits born of a deep freeze in 1990 that killed most of the California citrus crop. This pushed farmers into developing what would become one of the most profitable produce items on the market.

Global trade infrastructure allows for demand rather than season to dictate a fruit's availability. As long as shipping routes and highways remain open, grocery stores on the Alaska road system carry well-traveled citrus year-round. It's dizzying to hold an orange in Fairbanks and consider that it has traveled a greater distance than most humans do in a lifetime. To consider that yours are the last of so many hands to touch the peel, to toss it out a window or to miss your jacket pocket with your clumsy gloved fingers and drop it in the snow, a bright beacon from another world.

By the time I got to town, I couldn't stop thinking about how it was Earth Day, and the earth is warming, and we are eating citrus at an alarming rate in the sub-arctic. And of course I bought Cuties, because they are delicious, and so easy to peel.

First flower's last bloom

The earliest spring flower to bloom is the pasqueflower, a crocus-like blossom that splashes purple across still-brown southern slopes as soon as the soil thaws, while shaded areas and north-facing slopes might remain snow-covered. The blossoms are big and gaudy, golden stamen contrasting with the purple petals, and the season's first sighting feels like a gift. I can sit with them for hours in something between meditation and mania, watching ants, bumblebees, and, once, a spider, crawl between the petals.

I found the summers I spent guiding naturalist walks and educational programs awkward and tiring, rarely able to bridge the space between what I thought most interesting about a plant or animal and what visitors wanted to know. By the time the tourist season is underway, most pasqueflowers have gone to seed, wispy gray tufts easily lost in the newly greened forest, and after a few attempts to explain what they had looked like just a short week earlier were met with disinterest or confusion, I stopped drawing attention to them at all and eventually stopped this kind of work.

But I kept studying the flowers. I've challenged myself to look for them earlier each spring, rushing the moment of emergence. This means crawling in the wet decay of last year's aspen leaves looking not yet for purple but for the white fuzzy bud where purple will soon be. And then even earlier that that, looking for last year's blackened pasqueflower leaves, pressed to the ground by the snow's weight, and gently digging to find the bud the size of a Q-tip.

The pasqueflowers' brief season is one of melt and mud, when trails are punchy and unpleasant if not impassable, a season for staying close to home. One of my flower spots is the bluff overlooking the Nenana River where the Parks Highway crosses over it, about a mile walk from home or a stop on the drive back from the post office. Anything so close to the highway is inevitably doomed; a road is an insatiable monster once it's built. But still, I got attached, so when brush clearing for a new bridge and turn lane started in the spring, I crawled through the shredded trees and mud to see what grew anyway.

The flowers hadn't yet grown tall enough for the mower's blade to reach them, so by the time they were in full bloom, they towered inches above the layer of chipped aspen, a purple phoenix rising above the ash in water-logged miniature. I'd forgotten the details of the highway construction plan; I can only retain information about so many industrial projects at a time. More people traveling means more lanes, more bathrooms, more signage, more early morning backup alarms in the gravel pit next to the house. There is no arguing with the logic of expansion for the sake of safety. It was the last spring for some of these flowers. Sometimes little roadside non-landmarks are harder to lose than the grandiose.

After a dramatic January thaw exposed bare ground in a low snow year, I dug down to find the tiny white tufts, and then regretted it, feeling like I'd violated something. My neighbor Nan, a naturalist who taught me most of what I learned in my uninspired guiding days, told me the buds actually appear in fall and overwinter under the snow, which is why they're ready to bloom so early. Still, I felt like I'd violated something, seen something that wasn't mine to see. It was a relief when snow covered them again.

I'll keep checking the hillsides, looking for what survives each shift. Looking for signs any earlier than I have been, now that I know the buds are always there, waiting, seems like self-sabotage, like trying to name the idea of something before it's there.

A lot of spring is like that. A lot of creation is like that: a controlled wait, a flash of color, a sudden transformation into another thing entirely.

What would you do if you lived here?
I asked my friend's son, age six, "What's your favorite thing about visiting Alaska?" He's spent part of almost each of his summers here, visiting his grandparents, his dad's childhood home, the places that brought his parents together.

"Friends," he said, without hesitation. "And green." He's a desert kid, like I was, and I remember how exotic the claustrophobia of lush growth felt to me at his age. When I first came to Denali, even the scrawny black and white spruce of the boreal forest and its brushy understory felt like an enclosure, and I yearned for horizon, views above tree line.

At eye level, before you know how to see them, these spruce can appear sick, lower branches often bare and curled inward, live needles clustered on the upper branches, reaching for light. The boreal forest forms a wreath around the earth, or a halo. It is a forest defined by winter. I've come to think of green as an event rather than a defining feature, a hundred-day burst of willow and dwarf birch leaves, mosses, flowers, berries, followed by stillness when the snow comes. Spruce, of course, stay green year-round but depending on the light don't always look it.

As sunlight returns, it's easier to see which trees have been damaged in the last year. Spruce beetles have left a swath of brown branches in their wake to the south, and with warmer winters no longer keeping them at bay, the beetles are moving north.

At a community meeting about what to expect as beetles infested our neighborhood spruce, forestry officials offered tips on when to down beetle-killed trees (immediately, unless it's summer), how to protect a favorite tree from infestation (you can't, really, but there are things you can do to pretend, if you're the kind of person who has to feel that you've done something, like spray its trunk with a hose or shovel a protective cocoon of snow around it), and what can be done at the landscape level to slow the northward movement (nothing, really, the climate has changed too much to keep the beetles at bay).

Determined to come away from the meeting with a list of action items and unsatisfied with the message that it was already too late, the beetles were here, and our forest would be irrevocably altered in the coming years, a neighbor asked the forestry experts, "What would you do if you lived here?"

"I would be sad," one of them answered. I admired her candor, her unwillingness to cater to the too little, too late demands for action.

Green is often used to mean a set of values more than a color. It's too much weight for one word to carry and loses meaning in the metaphor. Ecology does not privilege one way of growing over another.

That said, there is nothing like the euphoria of a billion leaves unfurling across a hillside that seems to stay gray-brown longer each year in between the last snow and green-up or the first seedlings to emerge after the garden's dormancy.

Poetry doesn't pay

Cotton grass has always been one of my favorite northern plants, a mix of absurdity and grace. It's not a grass, and it's not cotton. I told Anderson, my friend's son who loves green, the name of the plant, and he asked, "What if it's actually just cotton cotton?"

I said, "Well, it's not." And he said, "How do you know?" And in the way of adults and naturalists, I said, "Because I know what it is, and it's cotton grass."

He proceeded to tear six of them out of the ground and "transplant" them three feet away, which I wanted him to not do, but once he'd done it, Craig said I should let him live his truth and not pluck them up and bring them home for my own decoration. I left them there because Anderson was six, and I am an adult and therefore a perpetuator of delusion.

I wrote a poem about cotton grass in college. It won third or fourth place in a university contest with a cash reward. For one day, I believed I could pay bills with poetry. The poem described driving around Anchorage with a man who showed me the construction sites he'd worked, mostly recently finished buildings where the plant life was starting to come back, including cotton grass. Thinking back on this, I'm not sure I correctly identified the plant, but the poetry judges didn't fact-check.

Years later, I wrote about permafrost for the National Park Service. I was one of five writers assigned an element of the landscape impacted by climate change, and as part of my research I followed scientists around one of their field sites on a network of boardwalk paths in the tundra. They'd set up boxes like mini-greenhouses to artificially warm small squares of tundra, and I learned that cotton grass is notable for its love of nitrogen-rich soil. In places where thawing permafrost released not only water but also nitrogen, which had previously been frozen underground and unavailable to surface vegetation, cotton grass thrived.

And then years after that, I got an email from a friend who'd been observing the profusion of cotton grass along torn-up trails where thawed permafrost can't sustain heavy use near her home, and at the same time she noticed a wave of social media posts commenting on the beauty of the new splashes of white bobbing tufts across the tundra. She searched online for an explanation connecting damaged tundra to thriving cotton grass, and my essay on permafrost was the first result. The research confirmed what she suspected: the increase in growth was a sign of warming. "I knew something wasn't right. It's fucking permafrost Armageddon out there," she wrote. "I have a hard time seeing this as beautiful."

I was paid well for that one. But every year there's more cotton grass, so I'm not sure which way the scales tip. Sometimes it takes me twenty years to finish a thought.

I don't know what to think about cotton grass. I don't want you to pull it up by the roots and transplant it, I don't want you to want more of it around, but if it's there I want you to see that it's beautiful. I want you to run your hands gently through the bobbing heads and giggle, mourn damaged trails, and demand action. I want poetry to pay more, though I don't write poems anymore.

Work ethic

We talk about the "lazy willows" as if summer is an assignment they've opted out of, the same branches on the same trees turning from green to yellow every Fourth of July, finding the photosynthesis endeavor not worth the effort. It's as if they're validating what we already know about midsummer: if the gloves and snow boots aren't put away by now, don't bother. Snow is on the way.

Six weeks later, the rest of the willows catch up, though that's a strange way to describe the change now that I've introduced the idea of laziness. Maybe it's the wrong word, the wrong concept entirely, to think of fall in terms of work ethic. Maybe what I want to say is I that I, too, want to find a way to relax in July, when ecological and capitalist cycles align to make laziness seem like wasted time, and sometimes the first yellow leaves feel like summer's pressure valve has been released. That the fleeting season when the yellows of willow, aspen, and poplar coincide with red dwarf birch in the mountains is my favorite, maybe partly because it's both ephemeral and draws a hard line: Summer is over. What's done is done.

Apolitical

I worked a few sporadic weeks as a community liaison for Alaska Fish and Game, calling my neighbors to arrange times to bring a state official to their houses and ask questions about their subsistence use. The state was, once again, proposing a natural gas pipeline from the North Slope to port via the Parks Highway corridor, and the law required documentation of how this massive development would impact food security and economies along the route.

The survey questions were designed for rural Native communities whose food systems are more intimately tied to the land, who do not drive two and a half hours to Fairbanks to load up the car at Fred Meyer and Home Depot once or twice a month. The Fish and Game biologist had never done this work in a predominantly white community, especially one with such a mix of professional federal salaries, short-term residence, little housing but dry one-room cabins, back-to-the-land sentiments, and seasonal artisanal bakeries. "It's very unusual to show up at a stranger's door in Alaska and say, 'Hi, I'm with the government, and I'd like to ask about your food harvests' and have people just welcome you in," he told me. He was unabashedly entertained.

The biologist and I shared our favorite answers after each interview:

> Question: If you weren't able to get the wild foods you harvested (salmon, halibut, fished in rivers or coasts hundreds of miles away), what would you eat instead?
> Answer, panicked: I don't know . . . store cow?
>
> Question: What would have made your year better in terms of harvesting wild foods?
> Answer: Hmm . . . maybe three to six bunnies (snare trapped).

Question: Did you harvest any caribou, moose, sheep, or deer last year?
Answer: No. I'm not very Alaskan.

Question: About how many blueberries did you pick last year?
Answer: None. No, four. No, not four gallons. Four. Wait, which ones are those? I'm from California, I don't know. Yes, I ate them.

One guy told us he ate a red squirrel—only one—either for the novelty or out of spite.

"You live in a funny place," the biologist observed. I agreed. After a few days of interviews, he told me he liked talking to people in any community, any demographic, about berries the most. "Berries aren't so political," he said. "Everyone likes talking about berries."

It's true. Secret spots, not-so-secret spots, canning methods, freezing methods, how to carry them in your pack on the way back down the mountain without smashing them to pulp with the pounding of your feet, look at these blue-purple stains on my pants/socks/fingers/baby's face, I want them to stay there forever. It's all apolitical.

Until you're confronted with an eight-hundred-mile-long pipeline corridor a mile from your house, and a gravel pit in your berry patch, and no promise that you or your community will get any of the gas but a lot of promises of more meetings about it, and then—

Come for the blood

Dwarf birch and bearberry leaves splash a quick flood of color across the tundra, lasting two weeks tops, then fade to brown.

Cranberries bunched in tight clumps picked just after first frost, or squished to red juice and licked from chilled fingers the following spring.

Something eating, or being eaten, blood splashed across the snow, fur or feathers blowing in the wind. Soon, scavengers come for the blood, too, cleaning tissue from bones and morsels of red-stained snow, leaving only squirrel tails, snowshoe hare feet, snapped flightless wings.

Red spots in the snow around women's dry cabins, unbothered shrugs: who hasn't been too cold or too unmotivated to get to the outhouse, instead marking a personal calendar since the last cycle, the last snowfall to clean up the yard.

Red is cyclic. Red is alive. Red turns us inside out, feeds us, reminds us what it is to be fed.

LAST ON THE DANCE FLOOR

1.

It's hard not to feel like the script has already been written. Yes, this is where I call the man into the bathroom to look at a pee-soaked plastic stick, I think, and I do, with some crass joke like, "Well, honey, I guess you had at least one sperm."

The small skulls and bones I've collected on hikes scatter the sink, the toilet tank lid. The lower jawbone of a marmot juts its two long, pointed teeth back at me. Fur and tissue still cling to the bone.

As a teenager, I would announce with adolescent conviction that nothing with teeth and hair was ever gonna grow inside me. Years later, it still seems like a reasonable rule.

2.

We make lists, perform the kind of visioning exercises I mock when others do them, live together in a haze as we wrap ourselves around the fact that our bodies have done this strange and mundane thing of which we had deemed them incapable. We weigh money against mortality against desire against time, and I say that the abstractions on his list frustrate me, that if it were a poem in a workshop, I would tear it to shreds. He reminds me that of course it is not a poem in a workshop, his eyes wide with sincerity. Hormones make me impatient, sarcastic, uncharacteristically practical. The possibility of life as a parent stretches out before me mostly in terms of unread books.

Later, telling a friend about our decision-making process, she says, "So it sounds like the main disconnect between you two is that you're frustrated that he doesn't think it's funny."

3.
My life is full of babies. I take auntie-hood seriously. I go to first birthday parties and elementary school dance performances, and not only because I live in a place where on an average winter Friday night there's nothing else going on. I love those kids fiercely. I love their parents. I love going home at their bedtime and pouring a glass of wine and opening a book and sleeping in so I have the energy to dance again with them the next day.

4.
(Do I tell you that to convince you I'm not deficient in my instinct to nurture, to love, to be the kind of woman a pregnancy is supposed to make you be? Or is it to say that I know what motherhood is, I know what a baby is, I have drawn henna prayers on pregnant bellies and held infants while their mothers broke down in tears at the wanted awfulness of it all, and it is an insult to those mothers and those babies to say that the darkened blob on the ultrasound screen was a child and the fact of its presence in my body made me a mother. No. It made me a mammal. Do not confuse the two.)

5.
Bears are the largest mammals to reproduce through the process of delayed implantation. Our local grizzlies mate in mid- to late summer. After mating, the fertilized egg divides once and holds in stasis for up to three more months, when the bear goes into hibernation. The female

grizzly's body self-regulates: if she hasn't put on the fat stores she needs to get herself and the possible cubs through gestation, followed by months of nursing in the den before spring, she will reabsorb the zygote.

Upon learning this, someone in every group of tourists always says wistfully, "If only humans could do the same thing."

"We can," I always want to say. "We do." We've just learned to call it something other than adaptation, learned to apply a set of laws to something that for bears is just necessity, a fact of life.

6.

The nearest clinic is in Fairbanks, as is the nearest grocery store, the nearest traffic light, the nearest decent restaurant open on the Sunday night before abortion day. We check into a hotel and go out for pizza. As our server clears our plates, she wants to ask for advice. "You look like responsible people," she says, "but like you also know how to have a good time."

She's twenty-two. She is leaving for six months in Utah before returning to Fairbanks, where she intends to live forever. She wants to know: should she sell her furniture or put it in storage?

Together, we conclude that either way, it won't matter in ten years. She'll either have the old furniture or not, and the agony of the decision will be overshadowed by life, continuing.

In the parking lot, I laugh. "See, love," I say, "fun, responsible adults can lose track of ovulation. And in ten years it won't matter."

7.

Abortion in Alaska is legal but logistically complicated. Everything is logistically complicated. Ending a pregnancy usually requires travel, which for much of the state means at least one flight, hundreds of dollars in addition to the cost of the procedure, and time lost trying to get all that figured out. It's nearly impossible to track how many people have tried and failed to end a pregnancy.

I have a lot in my favor. I have support. I have hashtags and a healthy sense of rage. I have a friend who offers a room so I can nap after the procedure while my partner shops for groceries and brings me pho in a Styrofoam bowl before the two-and-a-half-hour drive home. I live on the road system and have a working car to get to the clinic. I have a sugar daddy with a year-round job and a credit card.

"Don't say it like that," he says. "We're in this together."

"I know, love. Of course we are."

Of course.

8.

We get to the clinic early, and after all the pills and forms and waiting, the procedure itself takes less than ten minutes, and then I sit alone in the recovery room, underwhelmed, eating goldfish crackers. I think about how, when I lived alone, I used to buy goldfish crackers, and I don't anymore, but they're still uselessly pleasing. I add them to the shopping list.

It's ten degrees below zero when we leave, too cold for the protesters. I'm disappointed. I'd hoped to smile and wave as we drove off, maybe offer them a goldfish cracker.

(Goldfish are not mammals.)

9.

Two weeks later, I attend a typical neighborhood gathering, one where musician friends play cover songs in the community center and kids in socked feet duck between legs and under tables loaded with potluck food. I've been tired and cramping, sleeping early after substitute teaching, and this is the first night I feel social.

The band starts playing Gillian Welch's "Look at Miss Ohio," and I search for Kate, who is eight. Together, we join other childless women dancing with kids, and I lift her on to my hip. This is our song. She's getting too big to hold like this.

She's one of the first kids I've known since her birth, who I've babysat and rocked to sleep and yelled at and cried for, and who, at age two, sang a delightful toddler rendition of this song at the slightest suggestion. "Ooooh me oh my-ooooh," she'd croon tunelessly, smiling shy for the camera.

I ask her if she remembers singing it when she was little. She nods, and I hold her tighter.

We sing together, and I swing her at the line about doing "right, but not right now."

She and I will be the last ones on the dance floor. We will close out the night doing cartwheels with a teddy bear, and she will fall asleep in her dad's truck on the way home. I will walk home in clear, cold moonlight.

One day, I will tell Kate that we are doing right. Right now.

NOT JUST THE WOLVES

In the weeks on either side of the summer solstice, the sun barely sets and by 6 a.m. looks well on its way to noon. I worked three summers in a small lodge bakery, biking up the hill between four and six in the morning, and in those midsummer mornings the shift felt almost reasonable. But by the end of August, foggy twilight settles into the six o'clock hour, and by September, each day is six minutes shorter than the last, and soon the whole operation shuts down and I forgot that hours like four or six in the morning even exist. Alaska summer: it passes while you're busy doing other things.

On days I was the second to arrive, scones and muffins had already cooled under the oven. I arranged them in labeled baskets, made myself an espresso, counted out the register, and caught up with my coworker over NPR's *Morning Edition* or Pandora's classic rock station. I ate a misshapen cookie crumbled into steel-cut oats, checked the storage room for signs that squirrels had snuck in overnight. On days I arrived first, I chose the soundtrack; if I wanted news, it meant streaming a radio station from an earlier time zone until the rest of Alaska woke up.

Of course there was always some variable to the morning: a moose blocking the driveway, derisively eying my bike before stepping slowly out of the way, or the realization as I pulled off my rubber XtraTuf boots in the closet that I'd grabbed mismatched kitchen shoes in my rush out of the house, or jet-lagged lodge guests who forgot to order an early breakfast before their Denali bus tour and anxiously awaited coffee, directions, and a weather report before I'd processed the fact that I was awake.

Lodge guests filtered in for breakfast throughout the morning. I drew lopsided ferns in their lattes, bagged their lunches, and offered unexpectedly exuberant explanations of crepuscular mammals' latitudinal adaptations; we'd all worked as guides or naturalists before cycling into the service industry, and as grateful as I was that it was no longer up to me to get anyone safely from point A to B, show them an animal, and keep their feet warm and dry, there are some cues I couldn't resist taking even out of context.

I found it easier, for a time, to deal not in information but in caffeine and calories: buttery scones and kale and bacon quiches, foamed milk and extra shots. I liked the straightforward work.

The tourists brought the money, but the neighbors kept it real. They wandered into the bakery in twos and threes, stood too long at the counter, and still somehow forgot to pay: the National Park Service retirees, whose friendships have long transcended the jobs they once had, the pants-less toddlers whose moms snuck chocolate chunk cookies into their own bags, for later. We all undercharged Ron when he rattled up the hill in his 1926 blue-and-yellow Ford and helped himself to coffee refills when we were too busy or distracted to get it for him.

On one of the many mornings the phones were down, Linda burst in at 7:01 to ask what time it was. She thought it was two hours later and here she was, fully dressed, and all for nothing. I offered her coffee, given her situation as clothed and out of the house, knowing she only drank decaf, and only with company. She shook her head and went back home, either to take her clothes off or reset her clocks or I don't know what. She lived here before phones, before power lines, before artisanal bacon-date scones or Italian-style macchiatos, and now, like all of us, she resorted to swiping helplessly at a screen in a moment of uncertainty, rushing to the closest business for assurance that there were still other people out there.

Brad, the neighbor who supplied my first seeds when I started gardening took great interest in my struggling pea crop. He never dropped by to look at the stunted plants in person but walked his two golden retrievers past my house and up the hill to the café almost daily to nurse a single cup of coffee and a scone, speculating about what went wrong with this year's combination of heat, nitrogen, and microbes. "Go look," I urged. But he said, "Nah, I just wanted to come up here and talk about it," and slid his empty mug across the counter.

Jane shared tidbits of wolf management gossip, that cornerstone of Alaska politics, and told me who admitted unexpected sentiments about predator control or aerial hunting behind closed doors or on remote trails but would never tell anyone without a legislative majority, and we all know how unlikely that is, don't we. I'd leave cookies too long in the oven when Jane came in and forget to refill the creamer.

I'd forget this wasn't my house, and neighbors' kids weren't my kids when I reached across the counter to wipe boogers from their noses and then plate a cookie with the same hand, and then we'd all remember that this is food service and there are rules, but this is also a small community and a cool climate and little noses need a lot of help. I'd wash my hands too much one day and too little the next. When the cell signal came back, I hid in the back of the kitchen, sending emails I'd promised not to send to the wolf advocates, water overflowing in the prep sink. I was inefficient. Three summers in and yet half the time my latte art looked vaguely like genitals. I ate dropped cookies off the floor. We'd watch who came in together, and when Jane came in we'd tell her, too, about the unexpected coffee dates. She'd been around long enough to know it's not just the wolves that keep people around Denali. It's the gossip.

THE ROAD IS A WORD

I once wrote an imaginary break-up note in part to my partner but more to the place we live: "It's not you, dear, it's the highway: its infuriating linearity." I imagined the road as a cage. Its singular presence limits the imagination. Multiple roads suggest possibility: roads not taken, two roads diverging. Roadlessness opens the imagination further, to other kinds of travel.

One road, though, is a hard and fast line. One road is limiting. In certain seasons or some kinds of weather, when human-powered travel is restricted or trails are melting into slush, it can feel like a trap. One road is almost un-American.

But I stayed, and stayed, and that linearity became some kind of comfort.

The Parks Highway winds through the mountains from Anchorage and into the relative flat of the Interior to Fairbanks, across land where, once, only rivers and mountains formed boundaries.

Construction of the Parks Highway, first called the Anchorage–Fairbanks Highway, was completed in 1971, and like all major construction projects in Alaska, its story is told with a sense of industrial heroism. The highway, like the Alaska Railroad fifty years earlier, opened up the Interior. It roughly parallels the railroad, and like rail travel, revolutionized extraction, tourism, and travel. Roads and railroads snake across the continent, transforming the places they reach, their effects reduced to lines on maps.

Our scattered neighborhood, McKinley Village, lies a few highway miles south of the entrance to Denali National Park. The town of Healy, twenty miles to the north, formed around a cluster of coal mine sites and developed alongside the railroad in the first half of the twentieth century. Today, the open-pit mine, associated power plant, and the park keep the population around a thousand people. There's a grocery store now, and it doesn't feel new anymore. About the same distance to the south, the small village of Cantwell grew in the same decades, as Ahtna people moved to the area for railroad work and eventually stayed, alongside non-Native prospectors and trappers. Its population hovers around two hundred. It hosts a school with just enough students to stay open and the latest tiny restaurant we hope sticks it out through the winter months.

Our nebulously defined little bubble at the highway midpoint of what I think of as "local" is not a neighborhood in the urban or suburban sense of the word, where sidewalks and fences easily define property lines and the types of activities deemed appropriate between the boundaries. Most intersections along this stretch of highway are private driveways, marked perhaps with a sign, a traffic cone, or in one case, a stick horse planted in a five-gallon bucket. It's the kind of place where you can let yourself into your neighbor's house when they're not home and help yourself to a cup of sugar, where everyone's invited to a toddler's birthday party whether you have kids of your own or not. It's wholesome, a bit provincial, and a bit self-satisfied. Even in spite of the gravel pits, it is objectively beautiful: an expanse of spruce forest that gives way to rock and tundra in the mountains cradling us, and wilderness—both the federally designated kind and the kind that asserts itself simply by remaining undeveloped—that stretches out on both sides of the highway that brings people here and takes them away.

My neighbors are mostly white, mostly transplanted from elsewhere, and about half are committed to staying more than a few years. Few have been here long—one, maybe two generations at most. The highway predates most of the houses and the majority of residents. Some roads are named, but few are labeled, so not everyone knows them, and other markers stand in where a name isn't recognized. Some names can be traced to Dene words misheard by settlers and early National Park Service officials a century ago, repeated enough to take hold regardless. Other names can be traced only as far back as someone still living down the road or to jokes or references that that may not outlive the current residents. Karma Ridge, for example, refers to a bluff colonized by hippie environmentalists; Dead Dog Flats to a neighboring hollow where the winter cold sinks and stays, a microclimate ten to twenty degrees more likely to kill a dog than the surrounding hills. It can feel like a game, questioning each other and ourselves about creek names and who-lives-where, learning and repeating the names and landmarks, as if to establish our tenuous claims to this place.

Google Maps won't help you here, and most of us like it that way. The few roads that intersect the highway don't really go far, just to a few more driveways and clusters of houses. Our houses aren't numbered. There are no street addresses. We use visual cues to guide each other around the neighborhood:

"Do you know where the oil barrel lying on its side is?"

"No, but I know where the red truck is parked."

"Okay, so from there walk north, until you see an oil barrel . . ."

One fall evening a few years ago, the Department of Transportation erected a street sign at the intersection of the highway and the gravel road that leads to our house. An authoritative green rectangle now marks the turn: Old Parks Highway. It created a brief uproar about visibility, highway history, a community's right to name itself. This half-mile-long gravel side road is not, according to most mapped or anecdotal evidence, the Old Parks Highway, but instead the Old Denali Highway, which predated the Parks by about twenty years and followed a more circuitous route around the Alaska Range from the east, forming a section of what would become the Parks starting where the roads now intersect in Cantwell. Others remember it differently and remember a time when the old roadcut was referred to by the new name. One could argue that this doesn't matter. A road is a road.

Still, I fall squarely on the side of advocating for a nameless, numberless cluster. I joked about bulldozing the sign and nailing it to a different tree every night. Signs and numbers seem to detract from the illusion that we have to work to get to where we're going, that we're in a place that's different from the places we came from, where signs and numbers dominate the geography. When I first arrived, like many, I did not expect to stay, and like many, I did. I did not expect to develop opinions on lines and numbers or to feel quite so relieved by the lack of them.

I marked my home with a spruce tree and a rock and call it an address. I declared the day I arrived the baseline and call it history.

The American poet, novelist, and environmentalist Wendell Berry wrote, "The road is a word, conceived elsewhere and laid across the country in the wound prepared for it: a word made concrete and thrust among us."

Only this road, in this place, could make this kind of life possible.

Ghosts roam the highway.

Crosses and plastic flowers mark places where drivers fell asleep and crossed into the opposite lane, or overcorrected and rolled a car into the ditch, or hit unexpected ice. "Always expect ice," people say, and they're right. Every death seems personal: It could be anyone. It is anyone. I try to find patterns: times of day, known behaviors, demographics. Recently, three women around my age died in separate rollovers within forty-eight hours. "The highway isn't sexist," a friend assured me. I wasn't convinced, and I couldn't sleep the night before I had to drive to Fairbanks, reviewing fatalities by milepost and vehicle model. But there is no pattern. The highway takes randomly.

I find comfort in the prevalence of energy drink cans thrown out of windows along the local stretch of highway. It's a signal people are making an effort to stay awake.

During the annual spring roadside cleanup, neighbors have found sex toys, underwear, weed, and prescription slips. Despite the 350 miles between the small communities it passes through, the internet and the lack of other direct routes ensure that there is no invisibility on the Parks. If something has someone's name on it, it must have been an accident; no one would knowingly throw their personally identifiable trash out the window.

On a summer Saturday morning, a man driving a stolen truck from Fairbanks crashed into the trees just south of the Old Parks Highway intersection and took off on foot. News spread fast through social media and group texts: lock your cars, lock your houses, watch for strangers.

Craig and I had to dig for long-forgotten house keys, gauge which half-broken-down vehicles could start without intimate knowledge of their mechanical quirks, and then we took one of the running cars out to breakfast. We joked with the park ranger, guarding the intersection of the Parks and the Old Parks with an M16 strapped across his chest, about our broken cars, about the unlikelihood of criminal escape in a place with no backroads, no shortcuts.

The crashed truck and the fugitive thief were the talk of the restaurant, but no one let it get in the way of their Saturday morning eggs. By the time we headed home, the man had stolen a neighbor's bike, which someone recognized riding down the highway, and the thief was arrested in a pullout a few miles south.

The man had crashed the truck when he attempted to turn onto the Old Parks to escape Park Service law enforcement, who pursued him and the stolen truck at over a hundred miles per hour. He missed the turn and spun into the trees. If not for the road sign, would he have attempted it, or just sped past? The sign suggested an alternative, a possible road not taken. "That sign brings trouble," I said, half joking.

What, I wonder, could a desire for invisibility reflect? Mountains no longer function as natural boundaries; the highway passes through them. We imagine, perhaps, that unmarked roads are somehow protected from the progression of the history that makes our presence possible.

If, like Wendell Berry says, "a road is laid in the wound prepared for it," is damage to a road an act of healing or further injury?

Though it may be paved and repaved, the highway is subject to larger forces. Permafrost freezes and thaws and contorts the road's surface into tenacious heaves and bumps that, no matter how often the highway is resurfaced, return the next year. People share stories of a Christmas landslide that blocked traffic between McKinley Village and Cantwell and, more recently, a collapsing hillside that flowed across the pavement to the north. One year, after weeks of heavy rains, the Nenana River flowed so high it washed the southbound lane away in tire-sized chunks, *plop plop plop* into the churning gray water.

This road can be a reminder of the fragility of our occupation of this place, subject to the whims of water and ice and heavy equipment. Once, hunters followed game trails through the mountains, and settlers followed their trails, brought pack animals, mining dredges, dreams of pipelines the lengths of continents. Those trails became roads, and those roads came to serve desires: gold, oil, adventure, a nice drive with the promise of a warm bed at the end. More of us arrived, and our lives clustered around these roads. Maybe the desire to keep them nameless, to keep ourselves hidden, is partly a denial of our participation in a colonial tradition that, as Canadian anthropologist Hugh Brody writes, "sees the arrival and then spread of immigrants as the very purpose of history."

I count the mile markers, flower-laden roadside crosses, and frost heaves tracing the way home. I wave at the neighbors on the highway and always watch for ice.

And despite the reflective sign at the intersection of the Parks and Old Parks, the Alaska Atlas doesn't show a road here at all. Without headlights in the middle of a snowless night in early fall, the sign reflects nothing, its rootless words absorbed by the dark.

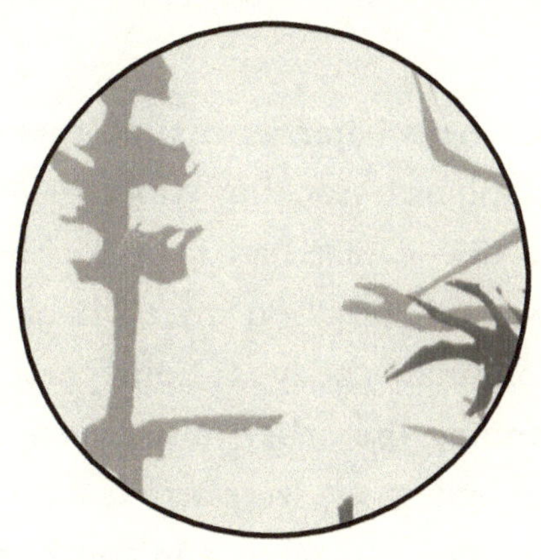

BOTTLE CAPS

I sold pins protesting the just-elected president at the 2016 holiday bazaar. Whatever you call the stage of grief where all you can do is smash bottle caps flat and glue his screaming face with a red line through it in the center and a craft store pin to the back, that's where I was. I didn't care if buyers wore them, threw them away, put them in a drawer, tossed them in the washer, or mailed them to a Republican aunt as a spiteful stocking stuffer—all of which they promised to do—I just had to make them. I displayed them in a wooden bowl on my table alongside decoupaged aviation map collages, flour tortillas, and sourdough bread, among the other housewives and hobbyists who wanted to believe we were artists a couple of times a year. In fact, some of us were, and some of us just had a lot of kinds of glue and time on our hands. We painted and glued and fermented our hearts out for pocket change, and every time we counted our cash over cocktails in someone's living room, we were surprised at how much time went into this and how little we had to show for it.

Two weeks before the bazaar, the same building served as our polling place. I'd spent the day with the rest of the election board—another gathering of mostly underemployed women—and we watched our phones with building dismay as election results rolled westward. Our precinct is a cliché, a little smattering of white greenie-commie-hippies-in-the-woods, politically atypical for the Alaska road system, where whiteness tends to correlate with more conservative votes than in rural majority Native precincts. Earlier that year, Alaska progressives had caucused in overwhelming support of Bernie Sanders. The Denali precinct held its first caucus, and voters from consistently conservative neighboring precincts joined in, and I'd helped do the paperwork for that, too, even feeling, for a time, a bit optimistic. But by the time the November election approached, it was clear this enthusiasm wouldn't translate to Hillary Clinton's campaign. I knew how Alaska's map would look by the end of the night. Between this and Alaska's position on the globe, voting here in a presidential election demonstrates a commitment more to process than outcome. Blue dot, red ocean, time zones against us, and a guaranteed cookie for every voter.

Still, I liked the process itself: a Sunday night reminder to the board to bring cookies to share with voters, setting up folding metal booths on their wobbly legs Monday evening, and a Tuesday spent highlighting names in the register and convincing each person, even if they say no one's gonna see them but their dogs that they need an "I Voted" sticker, and it feels like a wholesome victory when they finally agree. I even enjoyed the consistent redundancy of the paperwork: hand-count each ballot, two copies of everything, and in the case of a discrepancy, re-sort, recount, re-tally. It's tedious and human, and I can believe in humans even if I can't always believe in our institutions.

That night, we also had to tally local election results, school board and borough assembly seats. By the time I finally got home from the community center, two hours after Alaska's polls closed, Craig and my friend Jess had moved on from the cheap red wine I'd bought for its label—some kind of pantsuit pun marketing for the moment—to whiskey.

Half the year the community center is the closest thing to a public gathering place the neighborhood's got, hosting playgroups, local government meetings, movie screenings, knitting nights. Its walls are covered in faux wood panels and brown carpet, and decades-old water stains the ceiling. The adjacent fire hall houses two fire trucks handed down by larger volunteer departments. It's a utilitarian structure that tries to be little more than an enclosed heated space, nothing less. And on bazaar day, it's hot and crowded, kids stripped down to T-shirts and sweats and darting between legs, husbands of a certain age clustered near the door with cookie crumbs in their beards. It warms my heart and makes me want to scream, and I do it every year.

The pins weren't centered on my table, but they weren't hidden. A man I didn't know asked about my bread (organic flour, no dairy) and later I saw his wife whispering to him, and maybe she pointed, and they didn't buy bread, and I told myself I didn't care, but I still had the lingering small town want for people to like me. A ten-year-old kept circling back to touch the pins until, smiling to herself, says she wanted one for her dad, left again, and finally brought money and pocketed the thing like a joke between them, a joke I wasn't fully in on.

People started to linger at my table. A neighbor told me her gay coworker just bought his first gun. She said it like she was surprised. A woman who lived outside this blue dot said she was afraid to even go to the post office now, because "we've always known, but now we know the numbers." It started to feel like my table was a damn confessional: "I heard the n-word in town," they tell me, their white ears still burning. It was sad and awkward and our naiveté was almost funny. "I've been through two boxes of wine in ten days," someone said. "At least you can break down wine boxes," I offer, not like a winter's worth of beer bottles piled in plastic totes, the caps saved up for my "art."

A German woman I knew from ladies-only bunko games and her part-time job at the gas station approached, her eyes locked with mine from a distance. She reached across the table, grabbed a fistful of pins, and pushed twenty dollars into my hand. She leaned in, shook her fist. "We have our experience with people like these."

I didn't interrogate her use of "we," to ask if she meant women, or Europeans, or white Americans. I didn't look around to see who else might be listening. Her cash in my hand was a warning and a reminder.

I felt a chill. She kept looking at me. "You do," I said, making a choice about which "we" to acknowledge in the moment. "You do."

FIRE/LINE

The summer of 2019 was one of heat and smoke, local and national political upheavals, and sleepless nights. Drastic cuts to Alaska's education and healthcare were met with protests and legislative chaos. My work in environmental advocacy meant immersing myself in the Trump administration's extraction agenda rather than in the places we worked to defend. The sun hung in the orange sky like a dull balloon. But in quiet moments between rage, anxiety, heat exhaustion, and respiratory ailments, when I found myself alone with the smoke of 131 wildfires burning our forests and winding through the mountains and valleys to our front doors or fish camps or trailheads, I found myself having this *feeling*: a calm nostalgia, a wistful sense of the person I was, once, before I knew things I know now.

I first came to Alaska to work at Denali in the summer of 2004, which was a record-breaking wildfire year. For years, I'd speak and write about that summer but leave out the smoke, the chronic coughs and glazed eyes, the fact that on my first bus trip into the park, I didn't see anything but the hint of a distant horizon. I beelined with a stranger into the cold water of Wonder Lake because we couldn't stand the thought of another minute coated in the hot dust of the park road with no chance of rain. It can take decades to understand context. Memory is selective, and what I remembered best was the magic.

But senses are a bit of magic, too, and a scent memory will hold you. Fifteen years later, on the front steps of a friend's cabin in Fairbanks, a full breath of smoky air brought me back to my early twenties, to something of the unrecognized possibility that life stage held for me, and to my unabashed trial-and-error style of moving through the world. It happened again the next evening in my garden, after the sun dropped low enough that it was cool enough to work.

I laughed at it. I knew better. People were evacuating their homes. I must be delirious, I thought. *I haven't slept right in days because it's so hot.* Ash fell from the sky. My every action was impeded and second-guessed by paralyzing anxiety. Who was I to fondly remember skipping down a river bar in this unworldly golden light born of other peoples' forests burning?

But to give my younger self some credit, I was not without information in 2004. I understood that wildfire is an essential part of any forest's ecology. I was raised by wildland firefighters. When my dad brought home a giant sugar pine cone from a late 1980s fire in Northern California, I liked to breathe in the smoke smell it still held. When its scales closed up with each rain, even from where it sat on an inside windowsill, I learned that this was to protect the seeds the fire it was saved from could have released. That destruction was not linear, that life came from fire. I grew up averse to or inept at most physical labor, but rest assured, I played fire line more than house as a child, and I knew the ecological and spiritual value of regeneration.

I understood that the world was warming. Al Gore said so.

Pollutants, including smoke, travel. In the moment I was more caught up in the mystique of Siberian fires than those burning off the nearby Steese Highway, but my body absorbed the carbon of both from the wreath of smoke crowning the subarctic.

I knew, at least in theory, that oxygen deprivation can make you a little loopy. The list of what I didn't know is longer and well-trodden in the memoirs of every white lady who travels north and thinks she's found something. You can fill in the gaps. For example, I didn't know the actual realities of the places the fires burned. I saw only the smoke, not the flame. The places, like any places, were full of people and politics and dogs and bird eggs and tiny intricate mosses that might not even be named.

The political fixation with oil runs deep here, deeper than I could understand even hailing from another red state during the start of another endless war for oil. I hadn't really recognized the way extraction resembles religion, the way some believe oil drilling is synonymous with survival even as fires burn hotter and glaciers disappear and hillsides collapse in on themselves.

I didn't really get fireweed. Like, I got that, in a literal sense, it is a flower that thrives in disturbed soils and blooms bottom to top, but I didn't *really* get it, you know? The way it signals time, the way it tells you the land has been through something and is blooming, the way years and the months speed up, and suddenly you're talking mortality when you only meant to talk seasons and forest cycles. That flower can derail a conversation or a whole summer if you think about it too long.

More than six million acres burned that summer. (I had to look it up. And I'm spelling it out for you here so those words can turn around in your mouth, too, in case you, like me, don't really know what to make of a long string of zeroes.) It set records that 2019 didn't come near breaking with only 2.5 million acres burned by summer's end, even as other records were plowed down: the hottest days, the least snow, the earliest bloom, the most emails received asking for a legislative override of an Alaska governor's budget.

There were a lot of zeroes in that budget, too, and plenty of smart people laid out what each one meant, whose lives and livelihoods are hung in each vetoed digit. Look those up. I'm just here to figure out what to do with the smell of smoke.

There's a lot to be said for the early 2000s, the George W. years, the No Blood For Oil years, for my first view of hazy hills above tree line obscured by the ghosts of distant trees. I keep wondering: if the smell brings me back there, what can it offer me now?

I found myself turning to a lot of poetry about fire, which, unsurprisingly, is often also about politics, and, like fireweed, about death. And since the 2016 election, I returned often to Anna Akhmatova, the Russian poet who documented the Stalinist years in stark verse that's felt pretty resonant of late. After my late night gardening, the sun painted deep orange by smoke, I Googled fire poems again, and found one that I'd skipped or forgotten in the haze of the first Trump years, titled "July 1914." Akhmatova writes of a smoldering fire in a forest I imagined not unlike the boreal forest around me, bogs draught-dry and aspen leaves stilled in windless, smoky air. The next stanzas tell of a prophecy of terrible times, of violence and disaster, and then the prophet says:

> "But our land will not be divided
> by the enemy at his pleasure . . ."

In a later poem, titled by its first line, "I Am Not One of Those Who Left the Land . . . ," Akhmatova speaks of many of her contemporaries' exile from Russia and her own choice to stay despite persecution. She says that the flattery of the enemies of the land and people leaves her cold, and her songs "are not for them to praise."

And maybe in these lines, and the countless other poems, songs, and prayers that urge us to draw rage, heat, and creation from fire, I hear the lessons from the land and those who have long been its caretakers. I hear them urging us to stick it out.

And if the smell of the burning brings you someplace that draws out a bit of contradictory joy, let yourself have it. That's yours too.

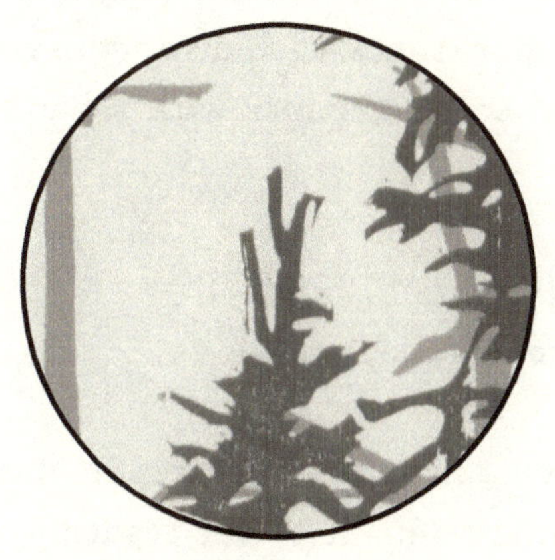

FIFTEEN STONES

My childhood best friend traveled to Rome with her family when we were thirteen, and she brought me back two film canisters, one black, one opaque white, full of small stones. I don't remember if I asked for this, or if she thought of it on her own, a low-budget souvenir for her friend whose family only traveled to the Midwest on vacation and who never studied Latin, who only knew about minor Roman gods if they'd been featured in a comic book. The black canister contained nine smooth, rounded gray pebbles and two chunky jagged ones, and the white canister, four stones, each distinct in color and shape, and a folded scrap of paper with a handwritten key:

Black—forum (center of Rome)
White—Colluseum (Gladiators)

Even now, I'm a bit pleased that she misspelled *Colosseum,* a lingering remnant of our academic competition. For a time we were inseparable and also unkind to each other in the ways of children and then in the ways of young women, and our eventual drifting was mutual and unremarked upon.

But even at my most carefree, I was too sentimental to live light. I carried with me every stone I was ever given. Gifts become harder to discard the longer you've kept them. The canisters sit on my desk. Sometimes I line the stones in a row, imagining the distance they have traveled from Rome to Arizona to Alaska, the shifting of friendships and rivers.

I still haven't been to Europe. I don't know if these stones I still hold were washed with the blood of enslaved fighters and then stepped on by generations of tourists, or if they were newly excavated from an ancient alluvial plain and transported and spread evenly across these well-trodden landmarks when my friend picked them up. I don't know if she knelt to the ground and chose each one like a flower, or if, rule-follower that she was, it was a quick bend at the knees, eyes to the sky, fingers grazing along the ground where she dropped, aiming not to be caught doing something that might be seen as stealing. I don't know much about Roman geology or architecture other than that it "wasn't built in a day," but then what is?

I do know that good gravel enables the kind of high impact, long-lasting infrastructure that defines contemporary notions of "development." It's a tradition that values ruins with a footprint and a skyline, roads with carefully constructed geology.

I live on land carved by glaciers and shifting rivers, and under what's now the surface are deposits of silt and rock broken down to rounded stone by water and into jagged chunks by ice. My front door opens within easy shouting distance of two industrial-scale gravel pits, where these deposits are mined and crushed and processed into two- and three-inch rocks, bought, sold, and made into driveways and parking lots and roadways. Here, gravel sinks into muddy potholes and melting permafrost and must be replenished if the guise of permanence is to be maintained. It's not cheap. You can easily blow a few hundred bucks on a single parking space. Gravel has a politics: Power lies in the ability to build a base. All other industry is ephemeral.

I've learned that there was a Roman god of boundaries and stones and he, too, required blood. The god's name, Terminus, also refers to the low end of a glacier. As the world becomes a less welcoming place for ice, most glaciers retreat farther into the mountains from which they flow. The rock and silt left in a glacier's wake has all traveled some distance to the place it is dropped. This is why the rocks in glacial rivers flowing from the Alaska Range are such an assortment of color and composition: they are an amalgamation of all the geologic processes that shape a continent.

Everything is always in some kind of motion. Anything built always tilts toward ruin.

Maybe it is Terminus, incarnate as an imagined future scholar of minute geologic discrepancies, who keeps me from tossing these stones onto our gravel road to blend with those that look just like them, to feed the insatiable potholes of a subarctic spring. He would note in these visually unremarkable Roman stones distinguishing traits not explained by shifting fault lines or glaciation but by the most haphazard of human movements.

I have built no altars and slain no goats, and I am not inclined toward prayer. I don't know if we were meant to take things in this way. I don't know what is mine to carry and what to return.

THE LAST TIME IT HAPPENED THAT WAY

A story about Denali National Park might start with a journey, logistics spun into allure by nearly a century of recreation managers, but after enough trips east and west, it becomes a story about gravel.

The Denali Park Road was built with traveler experience in mind more than practicality. It was built for settler culture's love of vistas, for gasps, for showing photos later, and for pointing out the steep drop and the long fall.

The route was a matter of contention: Why blast through mountains to snake a road along its side when a perfectly good glacial valley lay below, level gravel just waiting to be traversed by heavy equipment? But early park planners were adamant, and Horace Albright, then director of the National Park Service, would describe the final route in 1931 as "one of the most scenic highways in the National Park system."

Scenic is different than *beautiful*; beauty simply occurs, and a scene is contemplated, framed, and maintained. This road is studied and analyzed and fretted over. It is a myth laid down over mountains and rivers, and like any myth, it takes a certain suspension of disbelief to accept.

Polychrome Pass is one of the most dramatic stretches, where the road is carved into rust- and gold-colored volcanic rock, making a narrow shelf, or an open wound, blasted and smoothed into the mountainside. The National Park Service architects and directors in the 1920s chose the route carefully and deliberately, assuring themselves and each other that the work and money would be worth it for the view. Landscape architect Thomas Vint wrote in 1929, "The location should be made according to the best standards in order that as far as we can foresee we will have but one road scar in the park."

This pass demands near-constant attention: gravel hauled up from the Toklat River smoothed into its cracks and dips. Yellow-and-white equipment zigzags across the river, loaders piling rocks in dump truck beds. Half a million people a year can't get this kind of wilderness vista without a steady seasonal parade of diesel engines and steel blades.

Once, when I was visiting my partner Craig at Toklat Road Camp, where he spends summer workweeks away from our home near the park entrance, the only woman on the road crew told me about her ongoing efforts to save a mew gull nest from her less vigilant coworkers. "Damn hippie birdbrain," they called her, but they, too, avoided the nest, maybe because deep down they were birdbrains too, or they were scared of women, or both. Maybe those boys all knew she was a better driver than they were, fewer slips in the mud into the ditch, and fewer gulls dive-bombing her head when she got out of the truck halfway across the river bar to piss in the gravel, or to subtly relocate the GPS unit that tells the geologists where to tell the road crew to mine from. If the river doesn't replenish the gravel, the drivers are told to leave it alone; and if the gull's nest was made to look like a scraped out hole left dry, it made hatching just a bit more likely.

Those gulls made it. The river keeps pouring silty gray-brown water, gravel, and stone out of the mountains, and the glaciers keep receding. In the fall, when temperatures drop, the water starts to run clear, and you can look down into the flowing channels as easily as those the river has abandoned for an easier course.

Nothing remains intentionally untrammeled without an equal and opposite. When the eastern paved section of the park road needs repairs, materials and labor come from the gravel pit adjacent to our neighborhood near the park entrance. Up early each morning for summer bakery work, I'd hear the roar of the mobile asphalt plant stationed in the pit for the season, and once morning dark settled in again late in the season, the fiery glow emanated out of the pit across the neighborhood. Lodge guests asked about it, concerned. "Oh, that's just wilderness maintenance," I said, in my learning-not-to-give-a-fuck years. They didn't know what to say after that.

I spent an August evening watching the machine turn loads of gravel into smoking black asphalt, and a continuous procession of side-dump trucks carried it out of the pit, onto the highway, and into the park, where this nightly reeking and roaring residential terror would be smoothed into the mechanism for visitors' panoramic vistas east of Polychrome Pass. The gravel pit had been recently expanded, the edge carved out and raw, and I sat swinging my legs where tundra dropped off into the abyss, which serves as a sledding hill or informal shooting range when not feeding the industrial machine. Some of the biggest blueberries I found that summer grew at its edge, and as I watched trucks roll in and out, I moved slowly along the rim, popping the berries in my mouth until my stomach turned, maybe from too many berries, maybe from breathing the black smoke.

Heavy equipment gave Craig his path into the National Park Service. After years of working as a mechanic to fund a biology education, he was faced with a choice between low-paying, short-lived biology surveys or year-round work with benefits fixing road equipment at Denali. He went with the latter, doing heavy equipment repairs from the Toklat Road Camp in summer and the headquarters auto shop at the park entrance in winter. Summer months, he says he's got the best view one can have from under a broken-down dump truck. He ends each day coated in grease, welding dust in his hair, and in summer, he changes clothes at 5:30 and heads into the mountains for as long as daylight will allow. He can fix anything, I tell people, but would rather talk about wildflowers.

These are contradictions only to those with the luxury of imagining ourselves out of the equation. I've tried and failed to be a cheerleader for the pure abstraction of wilderness, but I always find myself drawn back to the in-between areas. If mine is a love story, it is as much about diesel engines and welding dust as the delicate bobbing petals of mountain avens above tree line or the way the mountains and valleys seem to roll on forever from a ridgeline barely wide enough to stand side by side.

My Toklat visits often fall during the in-between seasons, after the tour buses stop running but before all the work is done. Mid-September, after summer gigs wrap up and snow dusts the mountains, I head west against the flow of light traffic. My role, to the extent I have one, is largely domestic: to clean, cook, and pack, while Craig puts the auto shop and generators to sleep and teaches countless seasonal employees how to put chains on their Subaru tires. I bring hiking boots and a stack of books and try to stay out of the way.

The final exodus of the season includes most of the equipment used all summer to rearrange river rock into a road. One year, the scheduled departure coincided with the first real snow of the fall—heavy, wet snow that had barely turned from rain by midmorning—when the first to leave ended up walking the road ahead of their trucks and driving slowly in their own footprints. Those of us remaining in the west end of the park would form a convoy behind the only snow-clearing vehicle still on this end, a grader intended for other uses but ideal in that it was here.

I rolled my eyes a bit at the self-importance of the scurrying men making plans; the way I saw it, once you start calling yourself a convoy, you're already taking yourself too seriously. What we were was a line of eight vehicles snaked along the road, work trucks and personal cars loaded with a summer's worth of belongings, and me, along for the ride, mostly, but given purpose by driving Craig's Subaru back home so he could drive the shop truck. After a final scurry of last-minute mishaps—a parking brake frozen in place, a final pot of coffee before shutting down the generator, another cup of antifreeze down the drain—I found my place at the end of the line, eventually followed by two more pickups, and Craig at the end. I settled in for a long, slow drive, scrolling through my iPod at five-minute intervals for a playlist that fit the situation: nostalgic, energizing, familiar.

When our line of vehicles stopped moving at Polychrome Pass, the driver of the truck behind me said Craig had turned around to close a forgotten window in camp. We sat, idling. More snow fell. After several minutes of not moving, the grader operator marched past to the driver behind me, slicing his hand across his throat as he passed. The grader was stuck on a sharp corner ahead. The operator had felt the rear wheel slip, and his correction flung the weight of the machine outward, toward the cliffside. The front wheel slipped downward, and his telling suggested that he'd briefly said his final prayers, and then the wheel stopped, resting on the shelf accumulated from the previous week's load of river gravel dumped and smoothed into this perpetually slumping inside curve. The machine sat diagonal across the road. He was not going to try again. No one blamed him.

Men started important-looking pacing, because it's hard to feel important when your only real task is to sit in a truck and wait. Pacing becomes the only option. Craig's position at the end gave him freedom the rest of us didn't have, and after returning from closing the forgotten window he turned around again to the hill's summit for a radio signal. The only other woman among us, a firefighter I'd never met before, made coffee while crouched in front of her crew's truck, just ahead of me in line, shielding the stove against the wind sweeping up from the valley below.

Someone declared himself Incident Commander and announced that we were in "survival mode." I gestured toward my back seat at the contents of a fridge just packed into a cooler and the piles of bedding folded into the back seat. "I'll do my best to make it through with all this food and bedding," I said. Someone else played Angry Birds on an iPad. To each their own survival strategy. I joined these two and the woman who'd made coffee in the backseat of the diesel fire truck with its engine running, dug my knitting out of a bag, and settled in.

Kathleen Dean Moore says, "Domesticity is the central pleasure of the wilderness experience."

Some time passed before Craig informed us over the radio that he was digging his truck out of avalanche debris near where he'd turned to get a radio signal. Several of us shoveled a turnaround space, flinging snow into the wind and off the cliff or into each other's faces, and three people piled into the last truck to turn around and help dig Craig out. When they returned, Craig was giddy with adrenaline from his own variation on survival mode. His coveralls were so wet that when he took them off, they stood up without him as they froze in the back of the truck. He squeezed in to the back seat of the fire truck next to me, laughing at the adventure.

"You should make him a sandwich," the firefighter whispered to me, as if I were failing in my role as a convoy wife. "He knows where the food is," I hissed back, but then doubted my sense of scale: maybe sandwich making was, in fact, my only contribution. I made the damn sandwich, loaded with the end-of-summer remnants from Craig's fridge that I could dig out of the cooler in the Subaru. And we all sat in the fire truck for what would become a ten-hour wait for someone to plow us out from the east end of the park. Donner Party jokes wear off after about five hours. As darkness settled in, blowing snow swallowed the valley below us.

That slumping turn where the grader wheel slipped and stopped seems intent on shedding the road like an old skin. Each spring, the road surface slides down the hillside five, then eleven, then fourteen feet as the land beneath it thaws, and in more recent years, the thawing isn't limited to spring. Layers of gravel and canvas and more gravel are piled into the shifting edge, like Band-Aids plastered on skin over a broken bone. Basalt rocks tumble down from above; biking those curves in spring demands more faith in gravel than in gravity and offers good reason to question that faith. One year, after record-breaking heat followed by weeks of heavy summer rain, mud and rocks flowed across the road on these curves and elsewhere, and crews worked with heavy equipment and shovels to clear the debris. Maybe it's climate change. Maybe it's just one abnormality after another all year long. Either way it's a lot of work.

In Lima, Peru, in 2002, artist Francis Alÿs orchestrated and filmed a collective action titled *Cuando la fe mueve montañas*, or *When Faith Moves Mountains*. Five-hundred volunteers with shovels moved a sand dune on the outskirts of the city about ten centimeters from its original location. The volunteers, mostly students from Lima, wore white shirts and moved together in a line from one side of the dune, over the crest, to the other, moving one shovelful of sand each in front of them. Alÿs comments in the film that "the people who took part felt totally involved, and the fact that it took on such a huge dimension means that it will generate one story after another." The project's motto was "Maximum effort, minimal result."

The National Park Service is again considering its options.

A reroute is a diversion from what's considered normal, a deflection, a step aside or backwards. It would be a second scar, an admittance that gravity and warmth have won over government-curated grandeur.

Reinforcement or realignment of a melting mountain is more about denial than engineering. Bridges and tunnels fail regardless of climate.

And to admit that we cannot go as far as we once could is the kind of narrative Americans hate. A shortened road is a premature death. We all have a story and we all want to replicate it, again and again: Remember the time, right here, when something terrible could have happened but didn't? The time we rounded the bend and thought we might not make it, but we did? The tire almost too far into the shoulder, the rock that just missed? Go real slow. Watch the edges.

The edges are moving.
Go faster now, to keep up.
And STOP.
Maybe that was the last time it happened that way.

ACCUMULATION

The bear on the road's shoulder was not a surprise. Other cyclists had told us they'd seen him grazing in the creek bed, so my friend and I expected the small, dark grizzly pawing for roots as we rounded a bend. It was a warm, pleasant late May day on the Denali Park Road, before all the snow was gone and the summer season bus traffic picked up. The miles we'd biked that day climb gently from the Teklanika River valley to a tundra pass with a view of the Alaska Range, where we'd snacked and turned around, coasting back toward the river. When we saw the bear, we stopped at some distance and waited for him to move on.

It's important to follow rules around bears. Make noise. Don't run. Keep your distance. Stay calm. Look big. Wave your arms. They don't want trouble, either, and most of the time, once they know it's a human they're dealing with, they'll get out of the way. The National Park Service takes pride in Denali's excellent record of bear-human encounters: just one human fatality, a handful of interactions resulting in injury, only an occasional "problem bear" whose misbehavior is the product of human errors rather than its own. Often, it's young bears that get into trouble with their reckless teenage shit, testing the boundaries of their brushes with humanity.

So when this bear sauntered toward us rather than away, despite our shouts and waving arms, we switched into "stand your ground" mode, releasing the safeties from our canisters of bear spray and shifting the angle of our bikes as the bear approached.

"This feels like slow motion," my friend said. I agreed. The bear came closer, looked down at its feet in the ditch then up at us, its movements allowing what felt like an unnatural amount of time for observation and commentary. There is always something startling to me about a bear's eyes, a distance or void where I expect kinship. The earth completed a rotation with each one of the bear's slow steps. We shouted as if at a bad dog. My friend said, "If he puts one foot up on the road, I'm firing," and this seemed like a good plan.

The bear didn't step on the road but stayed on the shoulder, each long claw drawing its own pointed shadow. After it passed, we mounted our bikes and drifted down the hill in a numb haze. We each noted our lack of physical response: no increased heart rate, only an expectation that there would have been. Time readjusted itself. Just a few moments had passed. We warned others biking the road and flagged down a wildlife ranger approaching in a pickup. We told him that those before us had passed without incident, but that the bear tested us a bit, and if it's cumulative, we worried about what reaction the next encounter with hapless cyclists might bring.

"Well, it's all cumulative, right?" the ranger said dryly.

The word distance, as a noun, first appeared in written English in the thirteenth century, originating from Old French *distaunce,* meaning "dispute or controversy, civil strife or rebellion," though current usage is closer to the Latin *distantia,* or "a standing apart," or the space between. As a verb, it refers to the action of creating the space, of standing apart.

Before we saw the bear, my friend and I had been talking about the demonstrations for racial justice taking place around the world that weekend following George Floyd's murder. We talked about the distance we felt between us and any meaningful place to gather in solidarity, about the tensions and ease in our own dealings with law enforcement, about the presumption of safety with which we navigate the world.

The week after the bear, something happened with the stock market. Something is always happening with the stock market, and it's talked about in terms of bears and bulls. I can never remember which animal is supposed to mean which thing about stocks. Did whoever assigned these animals to projections about money know that bears act a lot of different ways?

The poet Alicia Ostriker defined metaphor as "a carrying across . . . that which joins, that which announces connections, overlap, shared essence, and yet retains the actual distance between whatever objects it brings together . . . . The distance, one feels, is infinite, all the winds of the cosmos blow through it. Yet at the same time it is zero. There is no distance, it is annulled."

It's easy to try to turn a bear into a metaphor, for sameness, otherness, strength, fear, confidence, vulnerability, an accumulation of threatening and banal indignities carried until something snaps. But usually, a bear is just a bear.

I already worked from home, distanced from my colleagues in Fairbanks and Anchorage, so when the world went into quarantine in 2020, a couple months before the snow melted and the road opened to biking, I felt prepared. Time and space had already blurred. We were well accustomed to Zoom calls and ended them now with cheery encouragements about hand washing.

The way a résumé stating little but a fondness for words and mountains can land a job picking Twitter fights with big oil companies is still a bit of a mystery to me, but it had. I wasn't bad at the work. As hospitals filled up and people poured into the streets in protest, the Trump administration kept pushing for more Arctic oil drilling, and I kept drafting talking points and press releases from my home office in the woods, double computer monitors displaying dozens of federal agency comment portals, grassroots actions, social media platforms, too many emails, articles, and climate data. My role was to distill complexity into narrative and write about it.

In his book Writing Tools, Roy Clarke offers refreshingly simple pointers for creating a desired effect in written work. He explains that a list of three things can achieve a sense of wholeness, a complete picture. Adding a fourth or more to a list achieves "escape velocity, breaking out of the circle of wholeness."

I crashed my browser weekly with too many open tabs, stories about melting permafrost, village relocations, wildfire, methane emissions from natural gas, corruption in the Department of Interior, dying salmon, Arctic solar battery banks, dying languages, absent sea ice, dying rivers, the role of hope in climate narrative, the role of personal air travel in global emissions, recycled wind turbine blades, dying birds, corruption in Big

Green organizations, the prevalence of chronic respiratory illness in communities neighboring oil and gas refineries, dying grandparents, global demonstrations for racial justice, Indigenous language revitalization, shifting tree lines, Alaska winter rains, the role of despair, the role of anger, the role of propane kitchen appliances.

Extensive lists can be overwhelming for a reader and should be used sparingly and with intention.

I attended webinars and meetings on narrative building and climate storytelling and my eyes glazed over, and after signing out of Zoom, I couldn't remember which browser tab explained story and which explained manganese mining. I often referenced a quote from journalist Quinn Norton I'd written in a journal, describing the difficulty of telling stories "in a world where falling in love, going to war, and filling out tax forms looks the same; it looks like typing." The word story started to lose meaning.

Take, for example, Scheherazade, the heroine of *Arabian Nights* who saved her own life and the lives of the women who would follow by telling a story so good that the murderous rapist king delayed killing her night after night. When we talk about the saving power of stories, perhaps it's the implied counternarrative that worries me: the idea that if Scheherazade were a less compelling storyteller, the killer would have won. What are we to think, then, of those who didn't escape? That they failed to get hold of their own narrative? Who has failed when the story saves no one?

Asked another way, is the goal to hold the villain king's attention in dazzled indefinite stasis while the world burns outside or to slit his throat and put out the fires?

Put a third way, I was losing hold of the narrative.

I reacted to the decision in August 2021 to close the Denali Park Road at the Polychrome slump with some relief. It came after days of heavy late summer rain, saturated hillsides and road shoulders, and flooding creeks. Calls and texts about the closure interrupted my endless scrolling through current and impending disasters. The immediate next steps were actionable, local, and relatively unimportant. The road is a low consequence microcosm.

Science writer and scholar Heather Houser suggests that writing about climate change often employs not only the same overused clichés and metaphors (wars and extraction are common; for example, canaries in coal mines, front lines, ticking time bombs) but also "tics," or less intentional patterns that signal a stagnancy in climate storytelling. Houser identifies one tic as the "catalog of despair," an extended list of impacts and disasters inserted into a narrative. She writes that the "catalog often comes in fragments or staccato declarative sentences in the present tense, situating the reader in the destruction as much as possible." On the scale of floods and fires, homes floating down rivers or collapsing into oceans, electric infrastructure outages, typhoons, salmon that don't come back or come back diseased, pavement buckling in the sun in a climate used to cool summer rains, a collapsed tourist road is not a catastrophic loss. But it was our non-catastrophic loss.

I might also write a catalog of despair to signal guilt about my relative comfort in the midst of collapse, to tell you that yes, I understand that this little melting road is not that bad, but I also understand the context in which it appears: look, look at this waterlogged map I have laid before you, and then at this other one, made of coal and ash. Sit with me, in the safety of our homes, as we memorize their lines before they fade. Someday we might need to retrace our steps along this road, to see if it still leads anywhere.

My friend Jess worked that summer as a backcountry ranger, and at the end of the day the road closure was announced invited herself over for wine and quesadillas. She'd spent the day calling everyone who held permits for the remainder of the season, telling them their trips would no longer be possible as planned. The rain was relentless. "So many angry people," she sighed, knowing the next day would be more of the same. Even those deeply aware of the climate crisis hate the *inconvenience* of it.

Her partner also worked at Toklat, and in more "normal" years, we'd sometimes drive out together, registering the purpose of our road permit use as "visiting boys." We awaited texts from "the boys" as plans came together, watched the rain, speculated on the possibility that the melting mountainside would become so heavy with water that it would give way in one sudden slide, stranding people on the west end of the park. I opened another bottle of wine. A part of me craved disaster, a tangible crisis that matched the sheer volume of emails and planning meetings about it.

The next few days were a flurry of other peoples' logistics, quick turnarounds, and ever-shifting end dates. I took time off from emailing and made one more trip with Craig to Toklat, and the day we drove the road west together the storm finally cleared. Fresh snow dusted higher elevations, mountains radiant against cloudless blue skies. We crossed the slumping curve, stopped on the west side and joked with the dump truck driver and the grader operator, watched as she dropped yet another truckload of gravel onto the sinking gray ribbon of road, and he followed, smoothing it over, as they'd been doing many times daily for months and would stop doing days later. As seen from the next bend, the melting snow highlighted the striped inverted arc of each previous road surface.

We'd built time for a walk into our schedule, as necessary a part of this pilgrimage as packing up Craig's longtime summer home. From Toklat Road Camp, we hiked up a ridge overlooking the river, far out of view of the failing stretch of road but part of the same ancient volcanic mountain the road skirts farther east. On the ridge, a dry tundra slope ascending into loose talus around three thousand feet, we were surprised by a newly exposed, narrow chasm on its north side, yet another place where the permafrost had melted, turning the mountain inside out.

We didn't know when this slide had occurred, other than that the last time Craig had hiked the ridge, it had been intact. He took pictures of me standing against the raw muddy wall, melting permafrost glistening in the afternoon sun. In some pictures I am smiling, as if posing at a destination I am pleased to have reached, and in others, I am squinting into the sun or in baffled annoyance at the camera, as if unsure if I am positioned for photographic scale or as witness to a tragedy, and viewed as a series it is clear that I did not know what to do with my face. We climbed a bit higher, a farewell meditation on a way of moving through the place that had brought us together. To the south, the Toklat flowed in two channels from the glaciers of the Alaska Range, converging into a single braided river on the south side of the mountain Craig and I hiked the day we decided to live together. The river continues north, opening up a wide valley flowing into Alaska's Interior. To the west, Denali glistened in the sun, the wispy clouds circling its peak, the only break in the blue sky.

The next day I drove east out of the park alone in a van loaded with Craig's food, clothes, camping gear. It was uneventful. He followed a few days later after a rushed wrap-up to his summer season. Two weeks after crews stopped dumping gravel on it, the road surface dropped several more feet. That winter brought record-breaking snowfall, Christmas freezing rains that weighted the spruce trees so heavily the tops snapped off when the winds picked up days later. When it melted, all those truckloads of gravel and time and effort lay accumulated at the ephemeral bottom of a still sinking hole.

Summer arrived hot and dry, bringing early wildfires and accompanying smoke. It wasn't until late June when I woke to the first cool, foggy morning of the summer, and breathing deeply while walking the dog in the driveway, I thought, "This reminds me of Denali summers," and with a sharp pang remembered the misty mornings of first summers here. I caught myself: I'd never left.

In her memoir of her youth and career influences, Rebecca Solnit writes, "Change is the measure of time, and I discovered that in order to see change you had to be slower than it." My own slowness sometimes knocks the wind out of me. I have learned that I can spend decades reflecting on the way the air smelled on a particular morning on a particular road, the way the clouds reached through the mountains like long feathered fingers, and look up to find that the mountains have melted around me, and no measurable precipitation has fallen in a month, and I am no longer young, and I don't know why I'm still standing here.

"Can we just sit with it a while?" I asked Jess. She spent many of her workdays at the new end of the road, talking to park visitors about climate change, unstable surfaces, smart route-finding, and bear safety. But I hadn't been there since my last drive from Toklat in the fall and sought some kind of closure or maybe a narrative opening. I wasn't sure. I'm still not.

Jess described how most people who walked the road to look at the hole that formed where the road collapsed didn't really know what to expect, but she enjoyed their conversations. For people who had never seen a glacier, it's hard to find meaning in being told that the narrow ribbon of white in the distance is one, and that it used to be bigger. Or if they'd never seen tundra, the idea that the willows growing along the shoulder of the road and snaking uphill in drainages are in any way notable is an abstraction.

But everyone understands that a road is built to sit on a stable surface and understands the force it takes to move it elsewhere. Jess talked to hundreds of people who walked the two miles, stepped up to the edge, looked down, then across the hole, and said, "Oh," like maybe they'd just connected some dots.

We dropped our packs. Jess perched on the metal toolbox next to the hole, adjusted her ponytail, and sipped some water. I crept closer to the place where the road dropped away, watched the wind whip a sheet of frayed black canvas, which, several layers down, was intended to keep the road in place and now flapped up from the void like a flaccid ghost attempting to climb from its grave. I recorded a video of the approach, then backed away and scrambled up the small hill above for a different view. In the hole below, the old road surface still held its shape, a cracked gray ribbon against golden jumbled talus working its way to the river.

It was a hot, windy day; the air was tinged with wildfire smoke from the north. Three days earlier, the Supreme Court had struck down Roe vs. Wade, and Jess asked if I still wanted to stick with our planned hike or "stay home and rage." I didn't have the energy to rage, but I had the energy to walk. So much of that summer felt like the predictable accumulation of what had already been mourned.

I'd walk to the hole several more times in the coming months, with visiting friends and family, making the two-mile trek from the bus to the unintended monument to a world in crisis and back again. There's always a certain kind of tourist who asks about every destination where the possibility of one is especially unlikely, "Is there a McDonald's out there?" and I tried to play the role of the other kind of tourist who chuckles politely as they pass. It was strange enough that this site of hours of labor, study, stress, and contemplation turned end of the road, turned temporary monument to a world in crisis, turned congressional budgetary line item had become, simultaneously, a destination.

Clarke lists the placement of "odd and interesting things next to each other" as another of his writing tools; for example, a collapsed government road through the wilderness and a ubiquitous fast food hamburger. McDonald's strikes me as such an in-between place, a pause on the way to something else, and maybe in that way they are a perfect pairing, a carrying across the distance. Maybe these tourists are on to something.

We climbed up and over the hole to the ridge above, and once there the wind carried our voices away and made it hard to stand still. We hurried back down to the sheltered roadcut on the other side. As we followed this familiar route west, the signs of abandonment were less dramatic: the road had narrowed where the hillside eroded below and debris piled on the inside shoulder from above, and rivulets of mud accumulated from small slides. The hard-packed gravel cracked and slumped, hints of what might collapse next. When we dropped to the valley floor, I scrambled into a patch of willows to pull out a ROCKS road sign that had blown from its signpost across the road.

A scholar named Maxwell Slater has, like Houser, identified certain tropes of climate change writing, noting how the writers are "always traveling places—from Antarctica to northern Alaska," places with which the writer in question is not often intimately familiar and writing about what they see: floods, fires, and famines, witnessed at a traveler's distance.

Familiarity, alternately, can breed a focus on the vapid. Yes, of course the glaciers are shrinking, but did you see that this sign Bob put up just last year has blown over and now he can't drive here to fix it? Isn't that just the silliest thing?

I'll be the one with my pack caught in the willow branches, fishing broken junk out of the bushes to make a point about how even the most attentive bureaucratic oversight can't slow the melting of the world, as the waters rise and the mountains crumble around me.

We walked a few more miles, then set up our tent just off the road, a novelty after years of following rules designed to maximize backcountry campers' sense of solitude: camp at least half a mile from and out of sight of the road, so those traveling on the road and off it can imagine themselves the only ones around.

That time of year, the sun is never gone long, and early morning it rose hot again. While I fumbled for my glasses in the overheated tent, Jess announced from outside, "There's a bear, headed our way." Still half asleep, I found my way out, bear spray in hand, and joined her in shouting, "Go away, bear!" Animals were quick to learn that summer that the road corridor was not the peopled place it had been before, and they took advantage of it. The bear stopped, paused to look at us, and realizing what it was seeing, took off in a bouncy gallop back in the direction it had come from. We boiled water for coffee.

The smoke, though still at bay, formed a gray wall to the northwest. We walked back to the bus turnaround, two miles east of the hole, along the braided streambed below the road, where everything looked more or less the way it always had. Except for the shrinking glaciers, the stream we walked flowed from and the expanded brush growth on the tundra. Except for the rock and mud newly accumulated at the base of the hill from the slide above. Except for the sense that every list has reached escape velocity, every story an act of mourning.

I have tried to follow the rules, to know when to stand my ground and when to back away, to list the proper number of elements at appropriate times, to leave certain stones unturned and paths untraveled. I have kissed at the top of the mountain and been pulled crying from the river. And yet. I have lost the stones I was carrying, the map I followed to get here. My hands are empty. The distance, one feels, is infinite, but closing in fast.

ACKNOWLEDGMENTS

This book has taken a circuitous route to its final form. Several pieces here have been written and rewritten, sometimes reshaped beyond recognizability, over almost fifteen years.

Many of them have been published in some form in the following journals and magazines. Thank you to those who helped them find their first homes:

An earlier version of "The Postcard Days" appeared in *Vela Magazine*, September 2014.

Passages in "Cordillera" first appeared in separate essays published in *Pilgrimage Journal*, Fall 2015, and *About Place Journal*, May 2021.

"End Words" appeared in *Cirque Journal*, Summer 2012.

A version of "Petty" was first published as "What We Know" in *High Desert Journal*, January 2018.

"Warranty" appeared in *Cutthroat*, Fall 2023.

"Shoreline" was published as "Love, Loss, and Water: A Meditation on Metaphor" in *ISLE Journal*'s Winter 2014 special issue on climate change.

A version of "Last on the Dance Floor" appeared in a now-defunct feminist journal. There was some drama. Perhaps you know the one.

"Not Just the Wolves" first appeared as "Caffeine and Community" in *Edible Alaska* online, May 2016.

A version of "The Road Is a Word" was originally published in *Panorama: The Journal of Intelligent Travel*'s Streetview series, August 2018.

"Bottle Caps" was published in *Tin House*'s Flash Fidelity series, May 2017.

"Fire/Line" was first written for the Alaska political blog *On Fire in AK*, July 2019.

"Fifteen Stones" appeared in *Panorama: The Journal of Intelligent Travel*, March 2023.

"The Last Time It Happened That Way," appeared in *terrain.org*, April 2021.

Many central ideas, if not yet the right words to talk about them, emerged during my time in the since-defunded University of Alaska Anchorage's low-residency MFA program, directed by David Stevenson and the late Sherry Simpson. There, I had the honor of studying with mentors Ernestine Saankaláxt Hayes, Nancy Lord, and the late Eva Saulitis. We built a creative community that still, despite the losses, has far-reaching tendrils. Thank you especially to Mary Kudenov, Lynn DeFilippo, Lu-Anne Haukaas Lopez, Vered Mares, and Annie van Dinther. Thank you to Michael Dinkel, for the letters and the fish; keep 'em coming.

I may not have come back to this manuscript if not for my time at Storyknife Writers Retreat. Thank you to Erin Coughlin Hollowell and Maura Brenin for creating such a generous gift of time and space (and food!). Thank you to my wonderful cohort, especially to Jamaica Baldwin, who asked a single clarifying question I needed to answer in order to move forward.

Alaska State Council on the Arts, Northern Alaska Environmental Center, Denali Education Center, and Fishtrap offered support that directly or indirectly nurtured this book.

I've had teachers throughout my life who have offered encouragement and a vision of what a writing life can look like. Thank you to Dawn Waggoner, Kim Holland, Patty Malesh, Mary Sojourner, Alison Deming, Luci Tapahonso, and Laura Pritchett, for your classrooms, writing prompts, reading lists, and more.

Corinna Cook, Christine Byl, Elizabeth Dodd, Malena Marvin, and Julianne Warren each offered valuable insights and perspectives.

Thank you, Emily Withnall, for offering such clear thinking and editing.

My parents, Kim and Val Watson, have never wavered in their support and in their love of wild places.

Thank you to my Little Birds: mutual validation, always.

And to the Denali community: Many of us have grown up together, whether we meant to or not. You've often been my first and toughest readers, my steadiest fans. For friendship, wisdom, and offering creative paths toward stability, I especially thank Nan Eagleson, Jess Toubman, Sarah Crowley, Sarah Stehn, Kim Arthur, Kate and NJ, Tom Walker, JBos, Anita Stelcel, Cassalyn and Nate, and the Knitters of Denali.

To Craig, for being my home.

Finally: This book is entering the world in a political era that may leave Denali and other national parks deeply changed, making these pages feel like a time capsule in more ways than I anticipated. This year, 2025, has already shown us the possible strengths of our connections to each other and the weakness of the systems of power that got us here. I find myself thinking almost constantly about the pasqueflower buds waiting all winter under the snow.

There is always more to say.

NOTES

The Postcard Days

The quote about "quiet reverence" comes from James Kari, "Names for Denali/Mt. McKinley in Alaska Native Languages," in *Shem Pete's Alaska: The Territory of the Upper Cook Inlet Dena'ina* (University of Alaska Press, Fairbanks, 2003), 211.

Byrd Baylor, *Everybody Needs a Rock* (Aladdin Paperbacks, 1974).

Cordillera

Edward Abbey, *Abbey's Road* (Penguin Books, 1979), 116.

Emery Cowen, "Protiva Gets Five Years' Probation for Blocking Trail: No More Monkeywrenching," *Arizona Daily Sun*, July 22, 2016.

Francis Alÿs, *A Story of Deception: Patagonia 2003–2006* (Museo de Arte Latinoamericano de Buenos Aires, 2006), 69.

Shoreline

Charles Wohlforth, *The Whale and the Supercomputer: On the Northern Front of Climate Change* (North Point Press, 2004), 150.

Annie Dillard, *Pilgrim at Tinker Creek* (Perennial Classics, 1974), 75.

Sheila Watt-Cloutier, *The Right to Be Cold* (University of Minnesota Press, 2015), 231, 241.

Cultivation

Frank Zappa, *Absolutely Free: The Complete Libretto* (Frank Zappa Music BMI, 1967).

Saul Alinsky, *Rules for Radicals* (Vintage Books, 1989), xviii.

The Road Is a Word

Since writing this piece, the Denali Borough installed street signs and implemented an addressing system. I've opted to leave that out, leaving a snapshot of a bygone geographical experience.

Wendell Berry, *Remembering* (Counterpoint Press, 2009), 96.

Hugh Brody, *Maps and Dreams* (Waveland Press, 1981), xiii.

Fire/Line

Anna Akhmatova, *Poems of Akhmatova,* translated by Stanley Kunitz and Max Hayward (Mariner Books, 1997), 59, 75.

The Last Time It Happened That Way

Quotations from Thomas Vint and Horace Albright can be found in "The 'High Line' Road: A Summary of the Decision to Build the Park Road into the Mountainside at Polychrome Pass," 2019-DENA-014. https://www.nps.gov/dena/learn/nature/upload/High-Line-Decision-6-24-2019-EJ.pdf

Kathleen Dean Moore, *Riverwalking* (Lyons and Burford, 1995), 45.

Accumulation

Alicia Ostriker, "A Meditation on Metaphor," in *By Herself: Women Reclaim Poetry*, edited by Molly McQuade (Graywolf Press, 2000), 157–58.

Roy Clarke, *Writing Tools: 50 Essential Strategies for Every Writer* (Little, Brown and Company, 2006), 101, 137.

Quinn Norton, "ACM Web Science Talk, as Written," quinnnorton.com, May 4, 2013.

Heather Houser, "Is Climate Writing Stuck?," lithub.com, January 3, 2022.

Rebecca Solnit, *Recollections of My Nonexistence* (Penguin Books, 2020), 32.

Maxwell Slater, "Why Write? Toward a Style for Climate Change," publicbooks.org, February 15, 2021.

ABOUT THE AUTHOR

Erica Watson is an essayist, writing instructor, knitter, and occasional community organizer living on the boundary of Denali National Park, Alaska. Her experiences in conservation advocacy, tourism, and environmental education inform her writing, which has appeared in *Terrain.org* and *About Place Journal*, among others. She is a graduate of the University of Alaska Anchorage MFA program, and a recipient of an Alaska Literary Award. Off the page, she can be found at ericarobinwatson.com, or hiking and skiing with her partner and dog.